Textures of Light

Textures of Light draws on the work of Luce Irigaray, Maurice Merleau-Ponty and Emmanuel Levinas to present an outstanding and ground-breaking study of the importance of light in Western thought. Since Plato's allegory of the cave, light and the role of sight have been accorded a unique position in this tradition. They have stood as a metaphor for truth and objectivity and the very axis of modern rationalism. More recently, however, this status has come under significant criticism from Continental and feminist thought which has stressed the privileging of subjectivity and masculinity in such a metaphor.

In *Textures of Light* Cathryn Vasseleu shows the ambivalent role light plays within philosophy. She challenges current interpretations of Luce Irigaray as an antivisual theorist by presenting her as a philosopher of both touch and vision. She also draws upon Merleau-Ponty's anti-Platonic claims for the corporeal and social context of the visual, and discusses Levinas's critique of light as 'first experience'. Throughout, the tension between vision and touch is carefully and clearly explored in a compelling re-reading of these often opposed senses that relates them to the texture of light as an organizing principle.

Textures of Light opens up new debates within Continental and feminist philosophy. It will also be valuable reading for anyone interested in visual studies and philosophical issues involving touch and vision.

Cathryn Vasseleu is a Vice Chancellor's Research Fellow in Philosophy at the University of New South Wales.

Warwick Studies in European Philosophy

Edited by Andrew Benjamin
Professor in Philosophy, University of Warwick

This series presents the best and most original work being done within the European philosophical tradition. The books included in the series seek not merely to reflect what is taking place within European philosophy; rather they will contribute to the growth and development of that plural tradition. Work written in the English language as well as translations into English are to be included, engaging the tradition at all levels – whether by introductions that show the contemporary philosophical force of certain works, or in collections that explore an important thinker or topic, as well as in significant contributions that call for their own critical evaluation.

Textures of Light

Vision and Touch in Irigaray, Levinas and Merleau-Ponty

Cathryn Vasseleu

London and New York

First published 1998
by Routledge
11 New Fetter Lane, London EC4P 4EE

Simultaneously published in the USA and Canada
by Routledge
29 West 35th Street, New York, NY10001

© 1998 Cathryn Vasseleu

Typeset in Perpetua by J&L Composition Ltd, Filey, North Yorkshire

Printed and bound in Great Britain by
T.J. International Ltd, Padstow, Cornwall

British Library Cataloguing in Publication Data
A catalogue record for this book is available from the British Library

Library of Congress Cataloging in Publication Data
A catalogue record for this book has been requested

ISBN 0–415–14273–3 (hbk)
ISBN 0–415–14274–1 (pbk)

Contents

Acknowledgements

I would like to thank Moira Gatens and George Markus for their generous and much appreciated involvement in the development of ideas that have culminated in this book. I am also indebted to Rosalyn Diprose, Linnell Secomb, Jodi Brooks, Elizabeth Grosz, Penelope Deutscher and Robyn Ferrell for countless vital comments and exchanges, and for extending to me their invaluable friendship and intellectual support. I would especially like to express my appreciation to Kate Gilroy, without whose care, humour and many insights the book would not have made it to the light of day. It has been a pleasure to work with my series editor, Andrew Benjamin, and with Adrian Driscoll, Tony Bruce and Katherine Hodkinson at Routledge. Thanks also to friends, colleagues and family who have given so freely of their attention and knowledge in the course of writing – Andrew Flatau, Judy Quinn, Anne Sefton, Jennifer Biddle, Margot Nash, Denise Robinson, Natalie Pelham, Margaret Ellis, Sue O'Connor, Linda Allen, Mary and Jim Vasseleu, and Tigger.

A portion of the text has appeared as 'Illuminating Passion: Irigaray's Transfiguration of Night', in Teresa Brennan and Martin Jay (eds), *Vision in Context*, New York and London: Routledge, 1996.

Part I

TRUE LIGHT

1

Introduction

Seeing light

The nature of light and existence are deeply entwined in the history of Western thought. Fundamental to this tradition is an image of light as an invisible medium that opens up a knowable world. In Greek thought visibility represents the ultimate certainty of a reality that must be confirmed visually. Seeing light is a metaphor for seeing the invisible in the visible, or seeing things in an intelligible form that holds all that exists together but is itself devoid of sensible qualities.[1] By means of this metaphor Plato implies a natural relation between existence and truth, or a concept of reality based on an original self-presentation of beings which can be clarified through vision.

In his doctrine of *anamnēsis*, or recollection, Plato makes a distinction between eternal Forms and their resemblances in human perceptions. The truth of the Forms is a light that has already been seen by the soul in its divine being, and it is this forgotten conjunction or participation of beings in the Forms which the incarnate soul recollects or is reminded of in the world it experiences through the senses. The union of the soul with the Forms constitutes knowledge, just as the union of the light entering the eye with light emanating from the eye constitutes seeing. Plato dramatizes the soul's recollection of knowledge in his allegory of the cave, where those who seek exposure to the truth must turn their gaze from the cave's shadowy and artificially lit world towards the sun as the origin of what can be known.[2]

In his study of the significance of light as a metaphor for truth in the Western metaphysical tradition Hans Blumenberg observes that in Plato's metaphoric usage light differs in nature from that which it evokes, namely the visibility of things (1993: 30–62). Platonic light is invisible and can only be 'seen' as *eidos*

3

(an idea, or sight with form) in the things that are made visible or brought into existence.[3] Rather than being a component of visibility, light has an originality of its own; it dawns with the appearance of things or the beings that come to light. In Plato's formulation light is the means of expression of truth's wholly exemplary nature, or a difference transcending the physical world and its history.[4]

Blumenberg identifies a change in light's significance that occurs with modern enlightenment thinking. Included in this change is the emergence of the idea of a history of light, where light's exemplary nature is no longer guaranteed but must negotiate its passage through darkness or the opaque materiality of sensible being in order to reappear. In this history light becomes either an objective to be accomplished, or an object at the disposal of the subject. Truth no longer reveals itself metaphorically through light. Truth is revealed in the ideal nature of light. Man no longer finds accommodation for himself in the light, or the fixed structure of an objectively perceived world; he himself becomes an emanative force. In modern enlightenment thought light is a realization of man's own nature that he brings into being in his transformation of the world.

In Descartes' theory of 'lumen naturale', or natural light, natural light has its source in God and possesses a perfect symmetry with the mind: 'For I have certainly no cause to complain that God has not given me an intelligence which is more powerful, or a natural light which is stronger than that which I have received from Him.'[5] With the notion of 'lumen naturale' Descartes hopes to bypass the vagaries of the senses. His study of dioptrics is based on the claim that a lux of non-sensory divine origin is the cause of movements of the lumen, or the light of the mind.[6] Natural light is seen in the action of a camera obscura, where the light coming from external objects can be projected on to a screen within the camera's dark interior to form an image, albeit with distortions caused by lens or screen. Jacques Derrida comments that for Descartes, while the existence of God is put into doubt, natural light is never subjected to radical doubt but rather is the medium in which doubt unfolds (1982: 266–7).

According to Blumenberg, in his idea of 'method' Descartes dispenses with light as an illuminating medium within which phenomena are viewed. Instead he treats light as a tool of reason by means of which phenomena can be subjected to examination, distanced and placed in perspective. The image of light as a tool is one that is prone to technological invasions: 'light turns into an encompassing medium of the focused and measured rays of "direct lighting"' (Blumenberg, 1993: 53). Heidegger also identifies a technologized relation between vision and light which he describes in terms of the ordering light of 'enframing', as opposed to a former openness of light which he evokes by way of the analogy of a forest 'clearing'.[7]

Blumenberg considers that the transition from illumination to idealization or 'lighting' culminates in a turn towards an artificial world reminiscent of Plato's cave. Within the modern technologized lighting of nocturnal spaces, 'an "optics of prefabrication" is being developed, which eliminates the freedom to look around within a general medium of visibility, and confronts modern man with ever more situations of coerced vision' (1993: 54). In signalling the possible end to its history Blumenberg articulates a longing and regard for metaphors of light as an elementary expressive mode used since antiquity as a means of tentatively grasping or intuiting[8] changes and differences in concepts in their unformulated first moments and multiple nuances: 'From its beginnings, the history of metaphysics has made use of these characteristics in order to give an appropriate reference to its ultimate subject matter, which can no longer be grasped in material terms' (1993: 31).

Rather than being a means of communicating immaterial concepts, Derrida claims that metaphors of light are constitutive of the language of philosophy.[9] Foregrounding the reliance of metaphysics on metaphors of light, Derrida names the metaphor of darkness and light, or self-concealment and self-revelation, as the founding metaphor of Western philosophy as metaphysics: 'not only because it is a photological one – and in this respect the entire history of our philosophy is a photology, the name given to a history of, or treatise on, light – but because it is a metaphor' (1978: 27). When Derrida describes the history of philosophy as a photology his emphasis is on light's metaphoric elaboration. The very condition of possibility of philosophy is metaphor, or more precisely the movement of metaphorization. Derrida argues that this movement is indistinguishable from the movement of idealization, or signification. He describes the movement as a double effacement, involving both the displacement of sensible origin and a forgetting of the metaphor (1982: 211–29).

While philosophy is based on metaphor, the concept of metaphor is itself dependent on metaphysics: 'Metaphor . . . is included by metaphysics as that which must be carried off to a horizon or proper ground, and which must finish by rediscovering its truth' (1982: 268). Derrida describes philosophy as a complex interplay of concept-metaphors which, far from being disposable or replaced by something more exact, are instruments that are inextricable from the field of philosophy which they constitute (1982: 228). For Derrida, light is the concept-metaphor by means of which truth can be made to appear or become present to consciousness. This light is conceived in terms of the sun:

> The very opposition of appearing and disappearing, the entire lexicon of the *phainesthai*, of *alētheia*, etc., of day and night, of the visible and the invisible, of the present and the absent – all this is possible only under the sun. Insofar as it structures the metaphorical space of philosophy, the sun represents what is natural in philosophical language.
>
> (Derrida, 1982: 251)

The structure of the metaphoric space inscribed by the sun is a specular circle or heliotrope. The movement of a heliotrope is simultaneously a movement turned towards the sun and the turning movement of the sun (1982: 251). In turning, the heliotrope returns to itself; it is interiorized without loss of meaning or expenditure. The heliotrope inscribes the law of metaphysics, which operates by reappropriating the conditions of its possibility.

Derrida extends the significance of this economy of metaphor into the philosopheme of heliocentrism which, he argues, characterizes the entire history of Western thought: 'The sensory sun, which rises in the East, becomes interiorized in the evening of its journey, in the eye and the heart of the Westerner. He summarizes, assumes and achieves the essence of man, "illuminated by the true light"' (1982: 268). Metaphysics is cast as the 'white mythology', which erases within itself the very conditions of its production, or its *logos*. In so doing, metaphysics not only reflects the culture of the 'West', but rises to its own mythological form, which is the universality of Reason (1982: 213). Light is associated with the imperialist cultural aspirations of 'white' man, or the man of metaphysical enlightenment for whom all that falls beyond *logos* is the indeterminate darkness that must be overcome and brought to the truth of a common (sun)light.

The sun is an exemplary natural object, entirely sensible or perceivable. Paradoxically, however, the sunlight of heliocentrism is also always partially artificial. On the one hand, the heliotrope is the paradigmatic metaphor, or model of the sensory sun. Being sensory, the sun is something whose presence cannot be mastered and is always improperly known. On the other hand, the sun is also always metaphorical, being the representative for all that is most natural in philosophical language. The sun is an artificial construction, which is not a bad metaphor, but a mere and infinitely substitutable metaphor of natural light: 'what is most natural in nature bears within itself the means to emerge from itself; it accommodates itself to "artificial" light' (1982: 251). As Derrida

6

describes the relationship, by metaphor we make things sensible, that is, both accessible to the senses, and sensible in an abstract sense (1982: 209).

The visible/invisible economy of heliocentrism is drawn by Derrida in terms of a filial relation. The visible sun is the analogue or son of the intelligible paternal sun which, as Derrida describes, is the hidden illuminating source of *logos*. The law of *logos* is capable of both blinding and protecting those who look within its scope.[10] Heidegger also identifies this double illumination in the Platonic redefinition of *eidos*, or idea. First, rather than the outward visible aspect of things, 'Plato exacts of this word . . . something utterly extraordinary: that it names what precisely is not and never will be perceivable with physical eyes'. Second, as well as naming the non-sensuous aspect of the physically visible, it 'names and is, also, that which constitutes the essence in the audible, the tasteable, the tactile, in everything that is in any way accessible'.[11]

Derrida argues that light is not just one metaphor used in philosophy, but the metaphor which founds the entire system of metaphysics or metaphoric truth. Luce Irigaray gives another inflection to the significance of light in the history of philosophy in *Speculum of the Other Woman* (1985a). Like Derrida, in this text Irigaray regards light as the founding metaphor of metaphysics. In 'Plato's Hystera', which is devoted to a discussion of the first part of Book VII of Plato's *Republic*, Irigaray considers Plato's organization of light and space in terms of the photo-logic of heliotropes (1985a: 243–364). However, rather than emphasizing the dependence of metaphysics on metaphors of light, Irigaray's attention is directed to relations of sexual difference in philosophy, a notion which, as Derrida proposes, sees itself in terms of a metaphorical light. Irigaray argues that the drama of concealment and unconcealment which is played out in philosophy's metaphoric labyrinth is an elaborate concealment of a maternal origin which is refractory to metaphysical conception. According to Irigaray, the fantasy which heliocentrism upholds is a masculine re-origination, or the appearance of giving birth to oneself – grasped self-reflexively through the mediation of light. By this means, philosophy generates a self-image while excluding any sense of its corporeality. Irigaray calls the light of heliotropes the light of the Same, meaning that difference is ultimately recuperated in the return of light from an intermediary point which is never present in language. Difference, which can only be figured as absence or invisibility, is ultimately reducible to an indiscriminate and overpowering light in which everything appears identical.

Irigaray's analysis takes up an aspect of metaphor stressed by Derrida; metaphor is both a means of passage to, and an inevitable detour or provisional loss of meaning in the arrival at, a proper meaning.[12] However, Irigaray places a different emphasis on the detour/passage of metaphor by relating it to the passage between the Platonic cave's artificially lit interior and the purity of the outside light. It is precisely the metaphoric omission of the passage which allows such movement that Irigaray protests.[13] Irigaray calls this avenue of transport the 'forgotten vagina', referring to its reappropriation in Plato's dialectic in an unnameable form. The 'forgotten vagina' is the 'passage that is missing, left on the shelf, between the outside and the inside, between the plus and the minus' (1985a: 347).

Derrida notes that in the *Timaeus* Plato nominates this excess as the unspecifiable *khōra* which defies the logic of *logos*, being neither intelligible nor sensible, yet cannot be separated from it. *Khōra* is an invisible that is devoid of sensible form or presence. While remaining alien to the intelligible, *khōra* both disrupts and participates in its constitution.[14] Irigaray's 'forgotten vagina' bears on Heidegger's interpretation of the term: 'Might *khōra* not mean: that which abstracts itself from every particular, that which withdraws, and in such a way precisely admits and "makes place" for something else?' (Heidegger, 1961: 50–1, quoted by Derrida, 1995: 147fn.). Irigaray contends that the 'in between' has no name in philosophy, which considers only absence or presence in terms of the Same. Plato is unable to speak of shadows inside the cave except as a loss of light in elaborate deflections and photo-plays. The perfect clarity of intelligible light is achieved as a progressive recovery from the displacement of light, which in the sensible realm is ambiguously differentiated from unrepresentable material obstacles, like the tain of a mirror, the bodies which cast shadows, the water's reflective surface, the cloth divider, or the walls of the cave.

While Irigaray makes much of the fact that Plato's metaphysics operates within a mythological cave which is analogous to a womb, she notes that various morphological features of a female body, including 'hymen', 'vagina' as well as 'womb', are essential features of Plato's myth. Of equal importance to Irigaray is the metaphoric re-placement of matter in the space of metaphysics. Although the Platonic drama appears to require no material support, such support is secured, or more precisely swindled, from the body of woman. For Irigaray, sexual difference is disguised by the attention focused on the reproduction of likeness by means of *logos*: 'whatever assures the functioning of difference in this way is always already foreign to the multiple action of difference, or rather differences, because it will always already have been wrapped away in verisimilitude, once the neck, the corridor, the passage has been forgotten' (1985a:

247). It is within this very process of limitation that the metaphor of *hystera* comes into play, with no representation of the means of passage itself. Metaphor displaces the fact that it obliterates the neck or transition, and the displacement is covered over in a matrix of resemblance.

The displacement of the materiality of the passage is the condition of possibility of circulation of family likeness between sun and son. In the course of mapping all differences within a system of equivalence, the dependence of the sun's offspring/filaments/images/rays on any material support becomes gradually more invisible. Eventually the materiality of light's reproduction is lost sight of altogether in the transparent light of day.[15] Light, the metaphor of resemblance, is displacement itself. The cavity of the cavern disappears after formerly being an eye socket with walls that conditioned the scope of the gaze. Vision enters a realm which no longer requires the human eye. Once penetrated by daylight the soul, which was formerly a mirror, loses its glass and its tain.[16]

In Irigaray's naming of Western philosophy as photology the weight of her argument does not fall on the elaboration of light as the founding metaphor of metaphysics. Her argument is directed towards the figuration of a complicity between photology or the language of metaphysics and the imaginary (phallocentric) male body.[17] She argues that this complicity is equally apparent in phonocentrism. While Irigaray argues that metaphysics perpetuates an imaginary male body, she is not claiming a causal or intentional relation between a biological or essential male body and philosophy. When Irigaray speaks of the body she is referring to its morphology – or a discursive reality which is irreducible to either material or cultural determination. Morphology is the form of a body as it is valued and represented, as it is interpreted and lived culturally. Irigaray sets out in 'Plato's *Hystera*' to make apparent the isomorphic imaginary body which philosophy constructs for itself, while it relegates the maternal-feminine to the role of securing that body's material conditions. In the course of this complicitous production, any form of feminine identity is effaced. Devoid of its own imaginary, the maternal-feminine is reduced to formless, mute, indeterminate, invisible bodiless matter which yields passively to the instruments of Man.

Irigaray's analysis of photology is of a metaphoricity which ensures that any engendering of maternal origin never comes to light. The continuous forgetting of sexual difference in the erasure of the materiality of reproduction is the very condition of possibility of metaphysics. With the re-origination of discourse through the metaphorical displacement of maternal origin the representation of feminine participation in reproduction is subsumed within an exclusively patrilineal economy, where it remains supplementary to a fantasy of masculine autogenesis. The exclusion is achieved in the differentiation between form and matter, in which matter remains the site of an unthematizable materiality. While masculine identity is formulated in opposition to matter, the feminine as matter cannot be thought. As Judith Butler explains: 'For Irigaray, the "feminine" which cannot be said to be anything, to participate in ontology at all, is – and here grammar fails us – set under erasure as the impossible necessity that enables any ontology' (1993: 39).

Irigaray pursues the trail of an invisible materiality which is systematically ignored in the adoption of a metaphysics of presence. Irigaray extends this assessment of the workings of heliocentrism to Derrida's naming of woman as writing or *différance*, where the identity of 'woman' is fixed as nothing but a trope for the undecidability of meaning. Irigaray argues that, just as the sun is metaphorically incorporated into philosophy, woman as trope of *différance* incorporates femininity while excluding any claim to a feminine identity by women. The trope of woman is an endless deferral of identity, independent of any material referent. In the idealist rationality of heliocentrism, 'woman' cannot refer to any woman in particular.

There is no nostalgia in Irigaray's assertion that the re-origination of discourse occurs through the metaphorical displacement of a maternal origin. Longing is a symptom of the interval between language and experience, or the crisis of the sign in which the gap between signifier and signified is expressed as nostalgia in modern Western culture. Derrida and others have diagnosed this crisis as the myth of presence of Western metaphysics.[18] By way of contrast the original claim which Irigaray articulates through her analysis of photology is that in essence *logos* is materially conceived, or reproduced. However, in the history of metaphysics the expression of any maternal participation in this reproduction becomes invisible or immaterial within the metaphorical reproduction of likeness:

> No proper sense, proper noun, proper signifier expresses the *matrix* of any discourse, or any text, even the legal text. The necessity of its (re)production is absent from what it lays out. Eclipse of the mother, of the place (of) becoming, whose non-representation or even disavowal upholds the absolute being attributed to the father. He no longer has any foundation, he is beyond all beginnings. Between these two abysses – nothing/being – language makes its way, morphology takes shape, once the mother has been emptied out.
>
> (Irigaray, 1985a: 307)

The ultimate target of Irigaray's reading of Plato's *Hystera* is photology's undisclosed erasure of its materiality, or the denial of any place in language for the mother to circulate symbolically. In place of that necessity is a language of desire that speaks of itself as Eros or a 'love' of *wisdom* that photology is singularly able to reveal. For Irigaray it is insufficient to acknowledge this exclusion as an internal fault of *logos* and conclude that the proposition of perfect specularity can never be entertained, as Rodolphe Gashé elaborates in his foregrounding of the materiality of signifying practices.[19] Irigaray's consistent argument is that such a language of desire for a thing which exists in denial of its materially reproduced nature is inadequate both to the representation of women's desire or to any sexually differentiated intercourse or erotic conjunction.

Within the borrowed light of an erased materiality Irigaray exposes the alchemic heat of a burning sun with the powers to inflame, destroy and transform flesh materially as well as to illuminate.[20] In Irigaray's words, photology stands as a 'heliogamy', or a deadly monogamous relationship with the fixed light of the Platonic sun which is 'disastrous for the still organic membrane of the eye: living tissue, unfit to receive the glare of such a fiery star' (1985a: 305). While Irigaray's project in *Speculum* is to retrace the movement by which the possibility of a maternal genealogy is lost in the dissemination of light, it is possible from her engagement in her work with Maurice Merleau-Ponty and Emmanuel Levinas, two philosophers who have interrogated philosophy's grounding in photology, to consider woman's participation in what could be called a 'genealogy' of light. A history of light refers to a course of events that can be traced in terms of the appearance of light, where light is regarded as the foundation or mythological source of these events. A genealogy of light refers to the continuous reinscription of light as a natural event, or light's origination as an always already present 'first light'. Rather than tracing the history of light's annunciation, genealogy attends to the traces or the material conditions of its articulation.

Textures of light

Irigaray's analysis of the erasure of sexual difference as the founding gesture of metaphysics is an undoing of photology that can be described as an engagement in the texture of light rather than in relation to light's value as either an ideal or physical medium originating metaphorically or naturally from the sun. A 'texture' is a disposition or characteristic of anything which is woven into a fabric, and comprises a combination of parts or qualities which is neither simply unveiled or made up. Texture is at once the cloth, threads, knots, weave, detailed surface, material, matrix and frame. Regarded in this way, light is not a transparent medium linking sight and visibility. It is not appropriate to think of light as a texture either perspectivally as a thing, or as a medium which is separable from things. In its texture, light is a fabrication, a surface of a depth that also spills over and passes through the interstices of the fabric. The dichotomy between the visible and invisible is itself a framing of photology that gives light its texture. As a texture, the naturalness of light cannot be divorced from its historical and embodied circumstances. It is neither visible nor invisible, neither metaphoric nor metaphysical. It is both the language and material of visual practices, or the invisible interweaving of differences which form the fabric of the visible.

A significant aspect of light's texture is that it implicates touch in vision in ways that challenge the traditional differentiation of these senses within the sensible/intelligible binarism of photology.[21] Conceived of in terms of this binarism vision has the distance required for theoretical knowledge and gives the sense of objective certainty and freedom, while the subjective immediacy of contact in the tactile faculty gives the sense of qualitative alteration and intuitive irrefutability. In its sensible indeterminacy as both feeling subject and object being affected, tactile perception is defined as a loss of objectivity in relation to the infinitude of vision's scope. The distance and space for reflection and insight that comes with vision through the mediation of light is lost as the sense of sight passes to the sense of touch. At the point of light's contact with the eye, the objectivity of the visual standpoint becomes a perception of the presence of difference, where light is experienced as a non-rational subjection to feelings such as being penetrated, dazzlement, ecstasy or pain.

In contrast to a hierarchical differentiation of vision and touch, it is possible to draw from Irigaray's work a concept of vision that is open to or affected by the touch of light. In her theorization of the relation between vision and touch, Irigaray argues that without the sense of touch seeing would not be possible. The indeterminacy of the body in touch is the basis of an erotically constituted threshold of immersion in the visual. Regarded thus, tactility is an essential aspect of light's texture, where texture refers not only to the feeling of a fabric to the touch, or the grasping of its qualities, but also to the hinges or points of contact which constitute the interweaving of the material and ideal strands of the field of vision. An elaboration of light in terms of texture stands as a challenge to the representation of sight as a sense which guarantees the subject of vision an independence, or sense in which the seer is distanced from an object.

Rather than founding a disembodied or objective visual stance, in its texture light has a corporeality which constitutes the dawning of the field of vision. The work which follows is structured around two of Irigaray's essays from which this theme can be developed. These essays, along with an introductory essay, 'Love of the Other', comprise the final section of *An Ethics of Sexual Difference* (1993a). The first essay is 'The Invisible of the Flesh: A Reading of Merleau-Ponty, *The Visible and the Invisible*, "The Intertwining – The Chiasm"' (1993a: 151–184), and the second is 'The Fecundity of the Caress: A Reading of Levinas, *Totality and Infinity*, "Phenomenology of Eros"' (1993a: 185–217).[22] My own reading of these essays will focus on Irigaray's rereading of the relationship between vision and touch in Merleau-Ponty's 'philosophy of ambiguity' and Levinas's 'philosophy of anarchy', both of which disrupt concepts of vision based on the assumption of a transcendental perspective. Merleau-Ponty recasts the body as an ontological question within the language of perception by elaborating its ambiguous determination in the intertwinings of vision and touch. Levinas considers a difference or an otherness that exceeds the totality of the visual, and in doing so challenges the privileging of the subject of light.

The nuances of Irigaray's differentiation of touch and vision are more apparent in her recent work than in her earlier analysis of the complicity between ocularcentrism and masculine identity in *Speculum* and the essays collected together under the title of *This Sex Which Is Not One* (1985b). Commentary on Irigaray's theorization of vision has been largely confined to this earlier work. As is well known, many theorists who have actively engaged in the issue of feminism in France, including Le Doeuff, Cixous, Wittig, Montrelay, Duras, Clement, Kristeva and Rose have drawn associations between ocularcentrism and masculine identity. Evelyn Fox Keller and Christine R. Grontkowski place Irigaray's work in the context of the anti-visual sentiments which emerged against what was perceived as a traditional privileging of vision in the Western hierarchization of the senses (1983).[23]

Keller and Grontkowski address this tendency to accuse the visual of being responsible for the logic of Western thought. As well as challenging the presumption of a hegemonic privileging of vision in the history of Western ideas, they also question the radicality of championing touch as a sense preferred by women, given that this distinction has a long tradition within which vision is generally accorded a higher status and touch a lower one. Keller and

13

Grontkowski argue that those theorists who consider that there is some inherent logic of the visual are ignoring that any such logic is the effect of an elision of vision and truth. Any correspondence between the visual and the intelligible is an operation of metaphoric (dis)association; between a mind's eye and the body's eye, between the sun and the purity of divine light, between the perception of sensible things and knowledge of abstract truths. Keller and Grontkowski interpret the association of the visual with objectifiability and knowability in terms of this dualism, rather than in terms of the visual. Descartes' radical division of mind and body is the ultimate expression of the logic of metaphoric (dis)association, with the intelligible activities of a knowing subject entirely separated from the passive mechanisms of a physical body. In objectivity the world is severed from the observer; in knowability communion is re-established through the mediation of light.

Keller and Grontkowski's analysis of the associations between scientific vision and philosophical truth also makes some preliminary suggestions about the de-eroticization of vision in the act of metaphorization. According to their analysis, the emphasis on the so-called 'objectifying' function of vision is achieved at the relegation of the communicative, or erotic, function to the realm of disembodied thought. They conjecture, by way of an alternative, that a conception of knowledge based on the metaphor of touch 'cannot aspire to either the incorporeality of the Platonic Forms, or the "objectivity" of the modern scientific venture; at the very least it would have necessitated a more mediate ontology' (1983: 221). This association of touch with a more mediate ontology, rather than in opposition to the predominance of vision, is closer to Irigaray's position on the relationship between a feminine sexuality and touch than is the common criticism that she reconstitutes a dichotomy between touch and vision.

Martin Jay considers this common criticism of Irigaray in the process of casting her as an antivisual theorist in his study of the modern status of vision, *Downcast Eyes: The Denigration of Vision in Twentieth-Century French Thought* (1993a). Irigaray and Derrida are grouped together in Jay's chapter on deconstruction and vision, in which he considers the two philosophers' analysis of vision in the context of their readings of ocularcentrism. The problem of ocularcentrism, as Jay presents it, is cast in terms of the relationship between feminism and deconstruction. Rather than conceiving this relationship in terms of a feminist debt to deconstruction[24] or the reverse, as Lyotard suggests when he acknowledges feminism's undermining of the symbolic as a metadiscourse (Lyotard, 1978), Jay considers the two philosophers' analysis of vision in the context of their readings of ocularcentrism. Derrida's work is not interpreted as a denigration of vision, but as a deconstructive position: 'it would be imprecise to call the suspicious approach Derrida does take to the primacy of vision in Western culture a straightforward "critique" of ocularcentrism' (Jay, 1993a: 496). On the other hand, Jay indicates that the general trajectory of his discussion of Irigaray will be the revelation of her radicalization of the 'antivisual components in deconstruction' rather than the deconstruction of ocularcentrism (Jay, 1993a: 498).

There is no denying that much of Irigaray's criticism is directed towards the privileging of the visual in Western culture, which she argues is tied to the perpetuation of a monological masculine subjectivity. For this she has been criticized for making generalizations based on her own globalizing reach, or her assumption of a prevailing phallocentric signifying economy.[25] There is a danger of interpreting comments by Irigaray, such as the following, as unvarying pronouncements of women's relationship to vision:

> Investment in the look is not as privileged in women as in men. More than any other sense, the eye objectifies and it masters. It sets at a distance, and maintains a distance. In our culture the predominance of the look over smell, taste, touch and hearing has brought about an impoverishment of bodily relations.[26]

However, with a different reading there is more to Irigaray's theorization of the visual than her analysis of the effects of privileging the gaze in a phallocentric economy.

Rather than radicalizing certain themes in deconstruction, Irigaray is attempting both a deconstruction and a feminist position which is irreducible to the terms of deconstruction. Irigaray is unable to choose between these two. To suggest that one can move inside and outside of metaphysics is to repeat the very division that it sets up. Irigaray's strategy, which she describes in the postscript of *Speculum*, is to insist on the two positions simultaneously.[27] I read this postscript as a key to Irigaray's methodological strategy of confounding an unavoidable systematicity by a double reading. Irigaray also makes a distinction between her approach in her earlier cultural analyses, where what is most apparent is that alliances are a necessary part of discourse, and *An Ethics of Sexual Difference*, whose style of alliances cannot be approached through an exhaustive decoding.[28]

In response to a question addressed to her on the implication of a woman deconstructing the 'theory of woman', Irigaray replies:

It is not correct to say that I have 'entered into' the 'theory of woman,' or even simply into its deconstruction. For, in that particular marketplace, I have nothing to say. I am only supposed to keep commerce going by being an object of consumption or exchange. What seems difficult or even impossible to imagine is that there could be some other mode of exchange(s) that might not obey the same logic.

(Irigaray, 1993b: 158)

While Irigaray is negotiating a place for the feminine within the representation of sexual difference, she is not trying to negotiate that place by resorting to the inverse of a masculine paradigm and embracing the absence of light, invisibility, and a distaste for looking as essentially feminine. Irigaray's efforts are not lost on Derrida, who comes closer to becoming open to such a position in his challenging of Levinas's ethics of alterity for its attempt to master sexual difference. Derrida portrays Levinas's mastery in terms of a textual sleight of hand which secures the origin of woman by substituting his own words in the place of hers (Derrida, 1991b).[29]

Irigaray is more ambivalent about vision, and Derrida is more in sympathy with Irigaray's refusal to embrace the Other of metaphysics than is shown in Jay's comparison of the two philosophers, set up as it is in terms of Derrida's ambivalence towards vision and Irigaray's antivisual stance. Jay concludes that, while Derrida is hostile to any traditional privileging of the eye, he is equally hostile to any hierarchizing of the senses or a radical rejection of ocularcentrism. On the other hand, Jay limits his consideration of Irigaray's rewriting of the assumption of undifferentiated matter to its negative implications for vision.

In terms of his intention to provide an overview, Jay's description of Irigaray as an antivisual theorist is more than justifiable. His analysis reiterates a prevailing assumption that she is exactly that. However, his analysis is also indicative of the absence of any different readings of Irigaray's stance in relation to vision. An irony of Jay's inclusion of Irigaray as one of the antivisual theorists against whom he argues for an ineradicable passion for the freedom of vision is that no opening remains for considering the extent to which Irigaray addresses illumination as an ineradicable passion.[30]

There is no discourse in existence of a feminine investment in light. In fact it would appear that light plays no part in the ethos of women. The following passage is frequently cited to demonstrate Irigaray's assertion that feminine desire is unrepresentable within the specular logic of Western thought:

16

Within this logic, the predominance of the visual, and of the discrimination and individuation of form, is particularly foreign to female eroticism. Woman takes pleasure more from touching than from looking, and her entry into the dominant scopic economy signifies, again, her consignment to passivity: she is to be the beautiful object of contemplation. While her body finds itself thus eroticized, and called to a double movement of exhibition and of chaste retreat in order to stimulate the drives of the 'subject,' her sexual organ represents *the horror of nothing to see*.

(Irigaray, 1985b: 25–6)

It is arguable that if Irigaray is asserting that touch is the unique preserve of female eroticism then her comment would be as prescriptive as the economy she wishes to subvert. However, to interpret this passage as representative of Irigaray's thoughts about female eroticism is to ignore the context in which she makes these remarks. Within this economy, which is *dominated* by the scopic, eroticism is consigned to the logic of an isomorphic imaginary. Woman is not excluded by the representation of this imaginary; her participation in eroticism is. Her body thus eroticized, woman embodies a desire for an invisible thing.

It is in this context that Irigaray's assertion – that woman takes more pleasure from touching than from looking – is made. The fact that woman must/cannot choose between the two is as much the issue which Irigaray is raising as her argument that the predominance of the visual supports an isomorphic imaginary. Rather than privileging touch over vision, Irigaray demonstrates in her discussions of both Merleau-Ponty and Levinas that touch is conceived of in terms of vision, as a source of mediation of a scopic economy. In each of her essays Irigaray takes up and extends the projects of Merleau-Ponty and Levinas in a way that neither philosopher is prepared or able to imagine, despite their intention to break with the visible/invisible foundations of Western philosophy. By way of contrast, Irigaray explores touch as a sense which defies reduction to the discriminations of vision. This does not make Irigaray an antivisual theorist. Irigaray has a regard for the indeterminacy of touch which invites a reconsideration of the constitution of vision.

Irigaray's approach to photology can be interpreted as a refusal to unquestioningly reproduce its logos or language of light. Irigaray chooses instead to transform the intertwining of the visible and invisible into an active political text. A positive commitment to vision is discernible in *An Ethics of Sexual Difference*, which is related to a more politically directed figuration of feminine visibility in the symbolic order. As Margaret Whitford describes the progressive

17

development of constant themes in Irigaray's work: 'she has moved from the stress on *un*binding, or *un*doing (eg. undoing patriarchal structures) to a stress on binding (eg. constructing new forms of sociality)' (Whitford, 1994: 381). Instead of simply seeking to place women's political aspirations in an intelligible light, it is possible to argue that Irigaray subjects this light to a radical doubt. While women's concerns are seen as unintelligible then photology stands as the history of a language that aspires to an intelligibility that has never existed. The issue that persists in Irigaray's rereading of photology is how the sexed nature of desires and political aspirations is incarnated or brought to light.

Part II

CARNAL LIGHT

2

Introduction to Merleau-Ponty

Merleau-Ponty's writing on vision must be located in the context of his claim that perceptual experience has a corporeally defined reality that is missing in empiricist and consciousness-based explanations of the interaction between a body and its world in perception. Empiricism construes the body as having a causal role in perception in so far as the body is regarded as an object from which responses are elicited. In consciousness-based formulations perception is reducible to the action of a thinking mind which exists as an external spectator capable of synthesis and reflection. Taking issue with the ideal viewpoint of a mind full of concepts, judgements and relations, Merleau-Ponty regards the specular as an essentially incarnate reality, bound to and produced within a corporeal and social context (1968: 235). Merleau-Ponty's account of vision is anti-Platonic. It inhabits a space which is tactile as well as visual, and is resistant to a unified, self-reflexive or panoptic viewpoint. Philosophers and scientists alike have traded, without acknowledgement, on the essential carnality of this sense. In his commitment to making a radical break with the privilege given to objective thought as the basis of knowledge Merleau-Ponty does not subordinate vision to other senses. Instead, he includes it in a general account of perception whose structuration defies reduction to disembodied or objective modes of consciousness. For this reason, Merleau-Ponty's work, with its insistence on the primacy of perception and, in later work, its questioning of the relationship between perception and language, offers itself as a unique interrogation and reinterpretation of both the nature of visual perception and the basis of Western philosophy's commitment to vision.

It is possible to identify two themes within phenomenologically redrawn visual schema that are integral to Merleau-Ponty's challenging of vision as the

21

locus of metaphysical speculation. The first of these is an account of light as a phenomenon that resists systematic idealization within the visible/invisible binarism of metaphysics, and the second is an account of an originary anonymous or impersonal, rather than reflective or intersubjective nature of vision. These themes recur throughout Merleau-Ponty's work but their significance is most specifically and originally addressed in his last unfinished collection of work, published posthumously as *The Visible and the Invisible* (1968). Merleau-Ponty makes a radical shift in his account of a phenomenological project in general and the corporeality of experience in particular in an outstanding paper of that collection, titled 'The Intertwining – The Chiasm'.

In this work Merleau-Ponty reconsiders his previous descriptions of the relation between embodiment and consciousness. From his earliest phenomenological accounts, for Merleau-Ponty the body is a locus of intentionality that is essential to all conscious experience. Here intentionality is understood as the ability of a body to direct itself towards, establish linkages with or act and locate itself in relation to a world, not as the action of a guiding consciousness. While committed to extending Husserl's phenomenological understanding of the body as subject, Merleau-Ponty is critical of the transcendental nature of Husserl's self-present embodied consciousness.[1] In terms of Lyotard's definition of phenomenology as 'that which appears to consciousness, that which is given' (Lyotard, 191: 32), Merleau-Ponty denies consciousness an intentionality which can be divorced from its embodiment in the world: 'My body is to the greatest extent what everything is: a *dimensional this*. It is the universal thing' (1968: 260). This is not to say that Merleau-Ponty attributes to the body a transcendental privilege that he denies to consciousness. His approach involves more than choosing between the two terms, which would be simply to preserve the dichotomous structure which is fundamental to Western thought since Plato.[2]

Merleau-Ponty's challenge to metaphysics begins with the development of the concept of the *entre-deux*, or the 'in-between two', which brings the excluded ground of oppositional terms into play. In his earlier works, this approach takes the form of demonstrating the fundamental undecidability of dichotomous terms. For example, in *The Structure of Behaviour* (1963) the concept of *Gestalt* is shown to defy simply either an objective status in physiology or subjective existence in psychology. Instead of opposing consciousness and the world as dichotomous terms, Merleau-Ponty attempts a tenuous and indeterminate synthesis between them. He describes the inter-

22

weaving of subjective and objective relations in positive terms, as a philosophy of ambiguity.

In his later work the concept of *entre-deux* is refigured as the concept of *flesh*. As flesh, the interwovenness of language and materiality in perception is embraced as an irreducible complexity that is necessary for a sense of self: 'flesh is not a contingency, chaos, but a texture that returns to itself and conforms to itself' (Merleau-Ponty, 1968: 146). According to Merleau-Ponty, the problems which he identifies as phenomenology's project in *The Phenomenology of Perception* are insoluble because his starting point in that work is the distinction between consciousness and its object (1968: 200). This distinction presupposes the perceiving subject and perceivable object rather than considering them as originating in a perceptual field. Merleau-Ponty recognizes the need to place the terms of his phenomenology under the scrutiny of a phenomenology which would challenge its own transcendental view.

In the working notes for *The Visible and the Invisible* Merleau-Ponty restates his project as the elaboration of an ontology or study of existence itself whose notions would replace those of transcendental subjectivity, including notions such as subject, object and meaning (1968: 167). The account of ontology as flesh is a profoundly ambitious recasting of the relationship between self and world, and self and other in terms of a language of perception. Not only would the terms of embodiment and experience change, but this language would also recast the way that philosophy could claim to perceive itself.[3] In contrast to philosophers who have challenged the adequacy of empirical schemas of perception, Merleau-Ponty attempts to define perception as existing in terms of a language of its own. Whereas Jean-Paul Sartre's criticism of any empirical schema of vision is that it 'could be as empirically adequate as I please, but it could never account for the fundamental fact that I see' (1958: 403–4), Merleau-Ponty takes up the fundamental nature of this fact as the starting point for his non-dualist ontology (1968: 3).

In *The Phenomenology of Perception* (1962) and *The Structure of Behaviour* (1963) Merleau-Ponty emphasizes the simultaneous participation of multiple physiological and psychological factors in the processes of perception. In *The Visible and the Invisible* his emphasis shifts to the articulation of a pre-discursive experience, or what he refers to as a 'deep-seated set of mute "opinions" implicated in our lives' (1968: 3). The aim is to elaborate within the terms of sensing the conditions of perception itself. That aim should not be understood as an attempt to rediscover raw data of perception, or the richness and immediacy of the perceivable world. As Irigaray and Lacan do, Merleau-Ponty theorizes the pre-discursive as the imaginary or unrealizable presumption of something's existence, never as the raw material of language.

Emmanuel Levinas contrasts Merleau-Ponty's approach to perception with a tradition of philosophies from Platonism to positivism which have attempted to make up for, or illuminate, what is considered to be lacking in the pure receptivity of perception.[4] For Merleau-Ponty, perception is a creative receptivity rather than a passive capacity to receive impressions. This creativity is an activity which is inseparable from its corporeality; likewise, incarnation in the world is inseparable from its capacity for such activity. Far from regarding its relevance as indefinable, Merleau-Ponty is determined to rediscover in perception what he refers to as the 'Lebenswelt logos', or language of the living, perceivable world: 'It is a question of that logos that pronounces itself silently in each sensible thing . . . which we can have an idea of only through our carnal participation in its sense, only by espousing by our body its matter of "signifying"' (1968: 208).

Merleau-Ponty describes the primacy of perception in terms of 'empirical pregnancy' or a productive signifying system in its own right (1968: 207). Modelled on his particular understanding of Saussure's diacritical account of language, this ontology displaces the mythological transparency of terms such as subject and object with an opaque differential logic of flesh. Compared to his earlier work in which the phenomenal body is the synergistic system or unifying source of the multiple aspects of perception, in *The Visible and the Invisible* the experience of embodiment is itelf schematized in the folds of flesh. This revision of phenomenological thought gives Merleau-Ponty a way of describing corporeality textually, as an engagement comprising multiple historico-cultural, ideal and libidinal dimensions rather than as something separate from or inadequate to them.

There are several aspects of Merleau-Ponty's account of embodied experience which, while not entirely successful in breaking with an objective notion of embodiment, are radical in their conception. There is a challenging of the division between the interiority and exteriority of psychical and physical embodiment and, related to this, an account of body image which is neither internally nor externally derived, but exists as an indeterminate interplay of both. Merleau-Ponty temporalizes embodiment in terms of visible and other modes of perception, introducing the idea of a fundamental contingency of meaning which challenges the nomination of any pre-given attribute, including sex, to a body. Instead, embodiment is formulated as the effect of precarious syntheses, or 'intertwinings'. Within the limits of some serious criticisms,

Merleau-Ponty's phenomenological project has yielded original and provocative analyses of embodiment among theorists in that area who have seriously engaged with his work.[5] Although he does not pursue the matter himself, Merleau-Ponty's revolt against disembodied consciousness is also a starting point for theorizing the texture of light as an irreducible nexus of language and materiality.

3

Living Flesh

Flesh

Flesh is Merleau-Ponty's term for the prototypical structure of all subject–object relations. In every instance of this relation, flesh defines a position which is both subject (a subjective reality) and object (objectifiable for others), and also simultaneously a subjectivity which is internally divergent with itself. In other words, flesh expresses the inscription of difference within the same.[1] Merleau-Ponty represents this structure in terms of one hand of a body touching the other hand – an example which encapsulates both the intertwining and divergence of flesh. The commencement of and participation in a tactile world occurs in the interplay between the two hands, each felt from within and simultaneously accessible from without or tangible for the other hand. Thus each hand takes its place among the things it touches, becoming a tangible being in the process: 'Through this crisscrossing within it of the touching and the tangible, its own movements incorporate themselves into the universe they interrogate, are recorded on the same map as it' (1968: 133).

The factor which conditions this relation is the reversibility of subject and object. A hand that touches is, in contact with the other, simultaneously an object touched. The two hands represent the body's capacity to occupy the position of both perceiving subject and object of perception. This example of the reversibility of tactile perception is regarded as representative of sensibility in general. However, it is not the body which is responsible for the double touching. The 'double touching' is the language of perception. The *body* is a term within flesh – it participates in so far as it becomes perceivable *only through its structuration as perceiving/perceived*. The body never perceives itself independently

26

of the language of perception, as a thing itself. It cannot exist independently of a thing perceived, but nor is it reducible to that thing:

> this reflection of the body upon itself always miscarries at the last moment: the moment I feel my left hand with my right hand, I correspondingly cease touching my right hand with my left hand. But this last-minute failure does not drain all truth from that presentiment I had of being able to touch myself touching: my body does not perceive, but it is as if it were built around the perception that dawns through it.

(Merleau-Ponty, 1968: 9)

By insisting that the body is not simply a locus from which we perceive, Merleau-Ponty takes issue with his own phenomenology of perception as well as transcendental theories of subjectivity which substitute the body for consciousness.[2] More importantly, instead of posing the body as the origin of perception, he poses the origin of the body as an ontological question within the terms of perception. At issue is existence as a being that expresses itself corporeally, or in its 'self'-production.

Living flesh is the modality of the body inscribed within sensibility. This body is not an internal or external projection, but a sensibility inextricable from its inhabiting of a world: 'things are the prolongation of my body and my body is the prolongation of the world, through it the world surrounds me' (1968: 255). In other words Merleau-Ponty transforms the concepts of interiority and exteriority into the indeterminate surfaces of a Möebius strip. Alphonso Lingis describes this as an inner face, which by prolonging itself becomes an outer face. Each aspect of the body has a variant outside itself (Lingis, 1977). In refusal of the mind/body distinction, Merleau-Ponty defines the mind as 'the *other side* of the body' (1968: 259). By virtue of its carnality, ideality becomes extension,[3] and by virtue of its ideality the sensible resides within the subject. Through sensibility (the double touching) my body inserts itself between the two leaves of the world, which itself is inserted between the leaves of my body (1968: 264). The body is therefore a hinge; an articulation of the world; an *entre-deux*. Alternatively, it is a fold – never reducible to the difference in which it is created.

As the envelopment of our double installation as perceiving and perceived in the world, sensibility defies the Cartesian differential dimensionality of *res cogito* (disincarnate thought) and *res extensa* (extended substance). For example, as Emmanuel Levinas says of pleasure and pain, both are characterized as an ambiguously mental and physically localizable experience (Levinas, 1990a: 61).

Merleau-Ponty gives the example of painting as an instance in which the dimensionality of visibility emerges, not in terms of subject and object, but as the emergence of meaning as flesh.[4] In painting, vision is not expressive of an object or idea; vision is expressive of itself – its flesh. In painting, the dimensions in which we see anything – 'invisible' idealities or concepts such as colour, line, contour, illumination – become visible in their own right.[5] A painting is meaningful as such only because vision is not explicable in terms of a look that reduces the image to a painted surface. Rather, it is only by going into the visible, or inhabiting the painting through a dimensionality which is sustained by the visible, that the visibility of painting can be experienced. Furthermore, through his analysis of painting, Merleau-Ponty underscores the profound intertwining of the cultural and the carnal in flesh. As the expression of the inner in an outer, living flesh is life as culture (Levinas, 1990a: 61). Painting actually destroys the illusion of disembodied spectatorship by basing visibility in its own carnality, that is by demonstrating that, even as it is his or her own, the seer's vision is the flesh of the seen.

One of Merleau-Ponty's overriding concerns is to provide an account of the commonality of perception that is based on the transitivity of an anonymously given intercorporeality. In the course of this undertaking Merleau-Ponty distinguishes the lived body from the physical body. He argues that the former is produced within an elaborate system of correspondences that collectively make up a perceptual field, and the latter is an object of biology. The lived body is a cultural identity produced within the perceptions that dawn through it, while the body that offers itself to biology offers itself as an object, not as flesh. Biology treats 'the body' as a thematizable object, moving towards an already abstract meaning. Flesh in contrast refers to the body as a living substance, or existence which must be assumed contingently as the condition for the expression of a point of view.

Neither subject nor object, but implicated in both, flesh is itself that which offers its body to biology as a thematizable object, or to art as an aesthesiological consciousness: 'Is my body a thing, is it an idea? It is neither, being the measurant of the things. We will therefore have to recognize the ideality that is not alien to the flesh, that gives it its axes, its depths, its dimensions' (Merleau-Ponty, 1968: 152). When Merleau-Ponty writes that flesh has no name in any philosophy, he means that it cannot be experienced as thought, or reduced to the theoretical (1968: 147). There is an ideality of experience or a sensing of flesh whose meaning is not grasped through concepts or conscious reflection but as moments which have a cohesion without the necessity of any formal unity or concept (1968: 152). The 'invisible' or ideality of flesh is the concept before it has become conscious of self, or a being whose existence resides in the language of sensibility. The body that cannot be properly conceived, adequately thematised or reproduced in thought is 'flesh'.

Reversibility – The Chiasm

Flesh refers to a body which is definable neither empirically nor abstractly, but in terms of its own divergence and reversibility. These two aspects of flesh are implicated together, or coextensive with and implied in each other. Reversibility refers to the body's simultaneous status as perceiving subject and object of perception. The reversibility of flesh can be incompletely 'grasped' or 'recollected' in its reflexivity. The touching together of two hands is the basis of reflexivity or the doubling of perception upon itself in a tentatively gathered precarious synthesis. Together identical in their difference, the hands constitute the body: 'every relation with being is *simultaneously* a taking and a being taken, the hold is held, it is *inscribed* and inscribed in the same being that it takes hold of' (Merleau-Ponty, 1968: 266). Although he uses touch as its exemplar, both hands mirror each other in their reflexivity. More accurately, Merleau-Ponty invokes the figure of two mirrors facing each other:

> where two indefinite series of images set in one another arise which belong really to neither of the two surfaces, since each is only the rejoiner of the other, and which therefore form a couple, a couple more real than either of them.
>
> (Merleau-Ponty, 1968: 139)

This image corresponds to the imaginary body which recollects itself, or persists through the doubling, like a glove that turns back on itself, or two segments of the same circular course, revolving from left to right from above, and from right to left from below (1968: 138).

Flesh is not a grasping of being in its reversibility but the inscription of difference in a chiasmic doubling/crossing. The chiasm is flesh in its intertwining, reversibility and its divergence or non-coincidence with itself. This gaping or spacing apart of flesh is the originary 'dispossession' of reflexivity's 'recollection':

> Consider the *two*, the pair, this is not *two acts, two syntheses*, it is a fragmentation of being, it is a possibility for separation (two eyes, two

29

ears: the possibility for *discrimination*, for the use of the diacritical), it is the advent of difference (on the grounds of *resemblance* . . .).

(Merleau-Ponty, 1968: 217)

In its reversibility flesh is only ever gathered improperly. The possibility of self-presence is dissipated in the divergence of perception from/within itself. Merleau-Ponty calls this a 'fecund negative that is instituted by the flesh, by its dehiscence' (1968: 263). This negative is not nothing. It is an unpresentable meaning which is expressed in the visible – as an intangible or invisible or silence which none the less we touch and see and hear.

The challenge of the chiasm for Merleau-Ponty is to gather, if incompletely, what comes of nothing, what comes out of the void. Chiasm is the name Merleau-Ponty gives to the motion of perpetual dehiscence, in which perception is understood as a being in momentum. This is a departure from perception understood as an object of subjective synthesis or as a pre-given schema determining the recognition of things. Merleau-Ponty makes full use of dehiscence as a generative term, taken in biology to refer to the splitting apart of fruits, seed pods, or organs to bring forth a flesh which differs from but is of their flesh (Stenstad, 1993). There is an interiority or depth of 'being within flesh' that comes to surface in the chiasm, as an opening of the perceivable world. The arising of sense is a 'fleshing out' of embodied existence, with flesh disclosing its (in)coherence or 'carnal meaning' in its differentiation of itself.

By means of flesh Merleau-Ponty describes the commonality of a language of perception that disrupts the idea of a self in possession of its own perceptions. Reflexivity is the body, always other in its reversibility. Reversibility is also the transitivity of that reflexivity as intercorporeality. Merleau-Ponty literally extends the body and its entre-deux into the communion and solidarity of self and other by transposing the motif of the double touching into the objective world:

> while each monocular vision, each touching with one sole hand has its own visible, its tactile, each is bound to every other vision, to every other touch; it is bound in such a way as to make up with them the experience of one sole body before one sole world, through a possibility for reversion, reconversion of its language into theirs, transfer, and reversal . . . all together are a Sentient in general before a sensible in general. Now why would this generality, which constitutes the unity of my body, not open it to

30

other bodies? The handshake too is reversible; I can feel myself touched as well and at the same time as touching.

(Merleau-Ponty, 1968: 142)

The other who feels or sees as I do in this extended reversibility is not an alter ego. It is not I who feel or see, but feeling and seeing are an anonymous sensibility which inhabits both of us. The concordant operations of the other's body and my own are one intercorporeal being, which supports a perceptual faith in a common world: 'this individual green of the meadow under my eyes invades his vision without quitting my own, I recognize in my green his green' (1968: 142). It is on the basis of this presumptive or imaginary domain opened up within reversibility that Merleau-Ponty theorizes a common world of humanity as 'one flesh' possessing an indefinite coherency in the weaving of relations between bodies.

The diacritical structure of flesh is rooted for Merleau-Ponty in the visual. The chiasm is metonymically related to the optic chiasma. This is an essential structuring element in the physiology of vision; in particular a means of constituting a stereoscopic image. As a physiological entity the optic chiasma is the point of cross-over of the fibres of the two optic nerves, so that the shared visual field of each eye is linked to a part of the brain on the opposite side of the body. Merleau-Ponty draws extensively upon this substantive account of visual perception in his account of the ambiguous ideality and physicality of the perceptual field. Carnal vision is stereoscopic in essence, not monocular. Monocular vision is the flattened, technicized vision of the disembodied transcendental subject or the mechanical eye:

> The binocular perception is not made up of two monocular perceptions surmounted; it is of another order. The monocular images *are* not in the same sense that the thing perceived with both eyes *is*. They are phantoms and it is the real; they are pre-things and it is the thing.

(Merleau-Ponty, 1968: 7)

The thing perceived with both eyes is real inasmuch as it has the dimensionality of sensibility, which is the diacritical reality of the chiasm. Physiologically, while it is possible to calculate distance with one eye (and we often close one eye in order to do so), the perception of depth (which gives a relational visual sense in terms of object and ground) requires stereopsis, that is a chiasm or crossing over of a double field of vision. This is not the vision which is simply the combination of two eyes, but an effect of a different order, created in the

31

in-between of the two. Experimentally, a double, not single delivery of stimulus is needed to elicit the effect of stereopsis by artificial means. Thus it appears that the resultant effect is not the product of a unified field, but instead is the *inauguration* of such an effect (a sense of 'stereoptic' unity) synergically. This doubling which gives depth-perception physiologically is synonymous with the ideality of dimension in Merleau-Ponty's language of perception.[6]

Paradoxically, however, the chiasm is out of sight. It is a dehiscence in/between visibility that is neither absent in vision nor properly visible. Derrida reads the fold of the chiasm as hymen in his analysis of Mallarmé's text 'Mimique'.[7] As hymen the chiasm describes the unity of the living body as a perpetual resistance to closure; a porosity subject to a leakage of meaning between figure and ground (Merleau-Ponty, 1968: 265). The hymen (also pharmakon, supplement, gram) is the figure of undecidability, naming the dehiscence, spacing, temporalization inherent in the consummation of meaning: 'it constitutes the medium in which opposites are opposed, the movement and the play that links them among themselves, reverses them or makes one side cross over into the other (soul/body, good/evil, inside/outside, memory/forgetfulness, speech/writing, etc.)' (Derrida, 1981a: 127).

Merleau-Ponty and Derrida differ in their understanding of the chiasm. In a reading which itself employs the figure of the chiasm, Mark Yount refers to reversibility as a point of contact and divergence between the two philosophers in their crossing over from dichotomous logic (Yount, 1990). Merleau-Ponty understands the chiasm corporeally, as medium of the enigma of sensible 'being'. Derrida understands the chiasm textually, as a supplement or figure of undecidability. For Derrida there can be no phenomenology of the chiasm or hymen. Reduced to a grammatological structure flesh would be deprived of a transcendental referent, or Merleau-Ponty's 'wild' or sensible meaning. Another way of describing the divergent positions is that for Derrida chiasm is an opening of a field of inscription that is the between of the text; the spacing or blankness without which there can be no sense of meaning (deferral). Chiasm for Merleau-Ponty is the diacritical spacing within meaning, so that a final sense is indefinable (*entre-deux*). According to Yount, Merleau-Ponty never gives up the quest to elucidate the stuff of experience, while Derrida reminds us that the last thing abandonable is the dream of an original signified.

In keeping with the figure of the chiasm, the distinction between the two philosophers is not really resolved by this comparison. Derrida has commented that, if one might argue that *The Phenomenology of Perception* falls within the metaphysics of presence or a belief in the possibility of coincidence between consciousness and being, with *The Visible and the Invisible* 'it is even harder to say'.[8] Far from being a matter for judgement, the problematic linkage between language and embodiment which is opened up between the two philosophers – between phenomenology's bodily text and deconstruction's texual body – is an immensely provocative one. Merleau-Ponty relates meaning to corporeality in the form of gesture – bodily expression – a gesturing towards an always unfinished articulation of a world. While itself unprepared to acknowledge the existence of perception,[9] deconstruction's reference to phenomena owes a debt to Merleau-Ponty's break with the concept of perception as a natural coincidence of consciousness and things. On the other hand, so to speak, from the perspective of deconstruction, the chiasm is textual and thus open to further division and reading.

When Merleau-Ponty refers to sensibility as 'empirical pregnancy', he is referring to flesh as a language of self-begetting. Merleau-Ponty has an image of flesh as birth. As Claude Lefort points out, in the passage: 'What we are calling flesh, this interiorly worked-over mass . . . has no name in philosophy' (Merleau-Ponty, 1968: 147), the word *'travaillée'* [worked over, wrought, elaborated] has a singular connotation in French, meaning 'the moment when a mother is about to be delivered' (Lefort, 1990: 5). Flesh is thus the double medium of being born and giving birth. Sensibility is itself the medium of its transcendence, the medium of its own emergence.[10]

Despite its metaphorical association with the maternal Merleau-Ponty resists the reduction of the chiasm to the female body. Merleau-Ponty's position is consistent with his description of the carnal body as never proper, but 'between the pure subject and the pure object a third genus [genre or gender] of being' (1962: 350). This genre is the anonymous gender of sensible being, or the one flesh. Neither subject nor object, male nor female, the chiasm is a structure of 'implication' (1962: 149), or a folding of opposites together so that they are also mutually reversed. This double enfoldment or invagination is the mutual 're-pli-cation' [*plier*: to fold] of differences in each other (Taylor, 1987: 71). The identity of differences is never established in this doubling/interplay of meaning. The coincidence of the chiasm is nothing more than a recovering, both in terms of surviving and concealing its gaping impossibility.

Derrida employs the chiasm as a figure of the undecidability of sexual difference. He does so in consistency with the meaning of chiasm as the absence of any fixed opposition, which includes sexual difference. The chiasm is an invagination that is neither/both inside/outside itself and cannot be said to exist, let alone have an existence that is attributable to woman. Hymen is not a distinguishable feature, and thus not a distinguishing feature of woman or man or even human.[11] Described in these terms, the gender of the chiasm is an impossibility which falls within the terms of Heidegger's characterization of ontological difference as an originary and asexual neutrality. This neutrality is not an absence of sexuality. It is a sexuality which does not carry the mark of sexual difference. It is the thought of sexuality as desire. Derrida names this neutralization as the enormous problem of attempting to think ontological difference and sexual difference (Derrida and McDonald, 1988: 180). In his account of carnality Merleau-Ponty does not attempt to address the problem. Chiasm is neither ontologically nor sexually distinct; it is in/between existence.

Rather than chiasm being sexually indistinct Irigaray pursues the argument that an unspoken fixture of sexual difference subsisting in flesh belies the notion of ontological difference. For Irigaray the dividedness of existence cannot be read reflexively in the case of woman, since there is no property of woman in existence. Instead Irigaray maintains that each being of woman is a materialization that differs in relation with itself such that no gathering of the difference is possible:

> So, when she touches herself (again), who is 'she?' And 'herself?' Insepar-
> able, 'she' and 'herself' are part the one of the other, endlessly. They
> cannot really be distinguished, they are not for all that the female same, nor
> the male same. That can be reassembled within some whole. This is to say
> again, or further, that it would be impossible to decide definitively which
> 'of the two' would be 'she' and which 'herself'.
>
> (Irigaray, 1991a: 90)

What Irigaray raises in her engagement with Merleau-Ponty is that an interior co-existence of different being(s) is not divisible phenomenologically. The difference of this interiority is a resistance to closure exceeding the (in)coherence of flesh.

Irigaray raises the question of whether Merleau-Ponty's configuration of difference is as radical as he suggests, or whether his non-dualist ontology can be criticized for allowing no space for radically other modes of existence. Merleau-Ponty characterizes the so-called 'enigma' or chiasm of perceptual faith as the presumptive domain which exists despite the impossibility of seeing things from the other side, or from a position in which one is not oneself implicated. This formulation problematizes the seeing of things from different perspectives, but not the different perspectives themselves. Although Merleau-Ponty notes that the senses vary in this capacity – for example, he considers

34

that the reversibility of sonority is more agile than visibility (1968: 144) – his principal concern lies with articulating the alterity of the chiasm in terms of visibility. In other words, it is the problematic of the reversibility of *visibility* which opens up the domain of perceptual faith, that is, the impossibility of seeing things from the other side. The formulation of alterity as an anonymous *seeing things* differently is less absolutely decisive than it first appears. As Merleau-Ponty observes himself, the reversibility of the 'sounding' of sonority, for example, is not arrested by the impossibility of seeing things from the other side.[12]

Rather than choosing the 'transcendental violence' of addressing the question of the alterity of the *other*, which would also be to introduce an irreversible asymmetry of flesh, Merleau-Ponty accepts the limits of phenomenological reflection and adheres to an originary perceptual dynamic as support of human communion. Here the motif of reversibility as a pre-discursive intercorporeal participation is represented as the connection between the chiasm of my eyes and the chiasm of the eyes of an other. Rather than rivalling my own gaze, the two gazes co-function as two identical organs of one unique body (Merleau-Ponty, 1968: 215). Merleau-Ponty's reliance on the figure of the optic chiasma of one body lends support to the equation of the reversibility of experience with the experience of a common intercorporeality. Lefort equates Merleau-Ponty's intercorporeal reversibility with Freud's condensation of the relations to the other into the functioning of an organ that is not only physiologically related but also bears the working of an impulse. In Freud's example, eating supports the impulse to swallow up external being, accompanied by the feeling of being at risk of being swallowed (Lefort, 1990: 10). In other words chiasm describes the experience of corporeality as a complex but ethically unchallenged movement of reversibility, vulnerability and incorporation.

Levinas discusses the common corporeality which is implied in the self-reflexivity of the hands of the same body as an imposition upon the radical separation of the hands of different bodies in the handshake. Flesh refers to an anonymous sensibility, not to a sensibility whose particularity is inadequate to universalization. Levinas's criticism of Merleau-Ponty lies with Merleau-Ponty's portrayal of intersubjectivity in terms of knowledge. The 'human' is constituted in terms of *knowledge* in the reversibility of flesh. The extension of the anonymous sensible qualities of the carnal into objective relations rests in the tacit agreement of parties upon things. This occurs in the face of a deficiency of knowledge of others. I cannot know what things are to them – I cannot see things from their side. Rather than being an overwhelming insufficiency, for

Merleau-Ponty the deficiency of knowledge is a positive characteristic of perception: 'I borrow myself from others; I create others from my own thoughts' (Merleau-Ponty, 1964c: 159).

Levinas refers to Merleau-Ponty's humanity of one flesh as 'but a moment or an articulation of an event of intelligibility, the heart of which is no longer situated within the human being' (Levinas, 1990b: 57). While sociality is constituted in the language of an anonymous sensibility, its consciousness is of the order of human knowledge. This formulation presupposes the constitution of intersubjectivity and problematizes the knowability of things. It is also not a sociality which admits much in the way of personal drama or differences of desire (Levinas, 1990b: 57). For Merleau-Ponty the intrusion of an other whose perceptual field will never be identical to one's own is not a radical contestation of existence by an other but means that the structure of all aspects of human existence must remain ambiguous in their determination and be experienced as being open to alteration. Taking issue with the intentionality of borrowing oneself from others, Levinas characterizes the relationship in terms of being hostage to the other, whose command of existence is an imperative that transcends and undoes one's own. However, as Edith Wyschogrod comments, Levinas's ethics is still parasitic on a presumption of the perception of both face and hostage (Wyschogrod, 1992: 234–5). While Merleau-Ponty's account of the body as the condition for world transactions does not admit of radically other modes of being, neither is the body simply a vulnerability.[13] As flesh the body is an unthematizable difference that is coextensive with its modes of orientation in the world.

Carnality

In *The Phenomenology of Perception* Merleau-Ponty argues the case for considering the body as an historical actualization rather than a natural entity: 'the body expresses total existence, not because it is an external accompaniment to that existence, but because existence comes into its own in the body' (1962: 166). Existence is not the a priori privilege of either a transcendental consciousness or body but is the mode which is common to the intertwined actions of the physical and the psychical.[14] Considered as an existential expression of intentionality, sexuality is integral to this body. In the chapter 'The body in its sexual being' (1962: 154–73) Merleau-Ponty describes how sexuality is neither empirically nor rationally determinable, but is a mode of embodiment that begins to exist for us through desire or love. In its capacity for sexual experience our affective life has a significance and reality which is not physically determined and not consciously chosen, but is the exemplary 'act of taking up a *de facto* situation' (1962: 169) or a human being that is unique to each one of us.

Merleau-Ponty takes issue with causal theories of sexuality which he argues isolate sexuality from its existential project. Where sexuality is regarded as a system of reflexes or drives governed either by their own necessity or by innate natural pressures, sexuality is detached from the impingement of an external world. Theories which regard sexuality as a learned response also divorce sexuality from external necessity by reducing sexuality to a mere representation or construct. For Merleau-Ponty, sexuality is inseparable from human existence. Sexuality is not reducible to the self-determining necessity of a drive, or a mechanism of nature, or a projected idea. It is reducible only to the intentionality of a body which actualizes its sexuality in conjunction with the world.

Merleau-Ponty begins his discussion of the body in its sexual being with a critical discussion of the case-notes of Schneider, a brain-damaged patient with a range of motor and intellectual deficiencies that various neurologists, psychologists and psychoanalysts attempt to explain in terms of tactile or visually based disturbances to body image. Among his symptoms Schneider demonstrates a loss of initiative or affective engagement in sexual activity which Merleau-Ponty argues is not explicable in terms of a visual or a tactile disturbance. He insists instead that in sexual activity vision, touch and abstract movement cannot be described as existing independently, but co-exist in reference to some form of internal correlation with each other. The fact that Schneider is unable to place himself in an erotic situation, shows no initiative in his sexual arousal by tactile stimulation and demonstrates no sexual interest in erotic images defies any single empirical explanation alone, such as psychological blindness or a primary tactile disorder. Neither of these theories can explain why both visual and tactile perception have lost their formal sexual significance for Schneider. Schneider demonstrates an asexuality in his visual and tactile comportment which Merleau-Ponty describes as the loss of an erotic perceptual schema.

As with the articulation of the living body, for Merleau-Ponty the realization of sexual functions depends on the emergence of a language of sexuality. Sexual meaning is operative, an otherwise imperceivable dimension of sensibility generated in an embodied relation with the world. Merleau-Ponty conceptualizes the libido as flesh in its passage from non-sense to sense. In this formulation, the unconscious is equated with the sensible, or flesh. As 'intimate perception', the libido is synonymous with perception as a language which we participate in intimately, corporeally. Sexuality and incarnation are inextricable. The ability to experience and participate in sexual desire requires a perceptual schema that is open to other perceptual orientations. A body with sense organs is necessarily a body that desires.[15] It is not possible to close the dimension of sexuality in the living body except by anaesthesia, that is, by the immobilization of the structure of sensibility and the loss of the means to experience affect. The libidinal body is the exemplar of the emergence of meaning in the anonymous circuit of flesh. Neither consciousness nor the unconscious are the source of sexual desire. Instead, both are conjoined in sexual experience as the very experience of the structure of incarnation.

In its being the lived body is a simultaneous dispossession and recollection. The libidinal body transforms this ambiguity into the adventure of eroticism. Eroticism is the denuding of one's substantiality, or yielding of the structure of one's corporeality to another. Alphonso Lingis describes the ambiguity which is sought out in erotic contact as a passage into the anonymous mode. To paraphrase Lingis, when consciousness and corporeality are no longer distinct, the carnal sense emerges. When consciousness is obsessed by its object, the spontaneity of the erotic verges on the brink of enslavement. Where the obsessive contact with the other is felt as the paroxysm of one's own feeling, the sense of the singular impulse veers towards a limit of equivalence. This is an encounter with an alien being, a denouement of individual existence into a predicament in which one is held. In the very process of its giving up its claim to meaning, the libidinal body exists as an affirmation of the non-sense of the sensuous, or what Merleau-Ponty calls the metaphysical dimension of flesh (Lingis, 1977: 344–65).

Lingis raises a criticism of Merleau-Ponty's adherence to a phenomenological standpoint in his account of the libidinal body as flesh. Lingis's criticism is directed towards the indistinguishability of erotic sensibility and sensuous sensibility in carnal intimacy.[16] The intentionality inherent in Merleau-Ponty's phenomenology is present in the account of the libidinal body. Lingis points out that the libidinal body never quite lets go of a hold on the possible, never entertains the scenario of being held by a presence that one has not taken the initiative of opening oneself to. According to Lingis, Merleau-Ponty fails to differentiate between sensuousness and voluptuousness, which is a being enthralled by the impossible rather than by the imperceivable. There is another way of stating this problem. Merleau-Ponty's account of sexuality does not admit a breach in the common experience of being as flesh. Sexuality is a passage into the anonymity of an undifferentiated sensibility, but it persists in its anonymity as it does in the singular, in a schema of divergence and reversibility. The anonymity of sensibility in Merleau-Ponty's description of sexual experience is the universal experience of the structure of incarnation. As a dimension of sensibility, sexuality is an anonymous mode of existence. The libidinal body is a sexually undifferentiated carnality that is simultaneously losing and taking hold of itself.

Although Merleau-Ponty attempts to describe sexuality in both concrete historical and corporeal terms his work has been criticized by Judith Butler for adhering to an objective standpoint in relation to the female sex (Butler, 1989). While embracing Merleau-Ponty's phenomenological description of the sexed body as a valuable intervention in the politics of sexual identity, Butler identifies a reversion to a more fundamental naturalism in his account of the genesis of sexual desire as a universal and natural form of human expression. Butler's critique of Merleau-Ponty's account of sexuality emphasizes the extent to which it is based on the assumption of a fixed notion of sexual difference. She notes Merleau-Ponty's innuendo that in so-called 'intimate perception' the female body exudes a natural attraction which elicits an appropriate response from the normal male subject. Butler claims that the body is objectified more drastically by intimate perception, where it is reduced to the erotics of an objectifying gaze, than by the objective perception which is the subject of Merleau-Ponty's broad critical project.[17]

In the context of sexuality, Butler contends that the reversibility of the body can be reformulated as follows: the body is an object to the extent that it is desired and it is subject to the extent that it desires. However, Butler concludes that despite investing the body with its own historicity Merleau-Ponty simultaneously limits the existential project of the sexed body to the world of a reified sexuality based on the heterosexual objectification of the female body. In relation to Merleau-Ponty's schema of intimate perception, Butler asserts that the female body denotes a natural object, and the body in general denotes existence. The inconsistency Butler identifies between Merleau-Ponty's phenomenological description of the body as self and his description of the body in its sexual being is that, while reversibility is the common feature of the body in general, this is not the case for the *female* body in its sexual being.

Irigaray takes up the issue of Merleau-Ponty's fixture of sexual difference in erotic perception in a different way from Butler. Butler's analysis refers to Merleau-Ponty's discussion of Schneider's (a)sexual bodily comportment in 'The body in its sexual being' while Irigaray concentrates on the attention

Merleau-Ponty pays to the significance of the interconnectedness of vision and touch in intimate perception as the very experience of the structure of incarnation. Rather than a reading of Merleau-Ponty's account of the erotic schema that associates the reification of the female body with the denial of its reversibility, the inherent reversibility of flesh in an erotic schema is itself an issue requiring closer scrutiny for Irigaray, and is pursued by her at length (as will be discussed in Chapter 5) in her engagement with Merleau-Ponty's account of tactility in 'The Intertwining – The Chiasm'. Merleau-Ponty refers to the body in its sexual modality only indirectly in this work, as a 'massive corporeality' preoccupied with the dimensions of its own desire (1968: 144). The body's erotic dimensionality is a latency in the sustenance of a perceptual field. Rather than dissolving away in the co-inscription of seer and visible with/ in each other, Merleau-Ponty describes an intimacy that is perpetuated between them: 'It is as though our vision were formed in the heart of the visible, or as though there were between it and us an intimacy as close as between the sea and the strand' (1968: 130). The subject of vision and the visible world have a co-existence in each other that is maintained carnally; held together in/ between an indeterminate contiguity.

4

Vision in the Flesh

The texture of phenomenological light

Merleau-Ponty's account of the primacy of perception includes a chiasmic reformulation of light that disrupts the dichotomous logic of the visible and the invisible upon which metaphysical thought is based. Light's essence in the experiencing of visual phenomena is rendered ambiguous by Merleau-Ponty's proposition of the corporeality of all conscious experience. In place of a distinction between the visible (sensible experience or perception) and the invisible (intelligible laws or thought), Merleau-Ponty gives an account of the embodied nature of both visible and invisible light. The fantasy of intelligible light is that it exists in its own terms independently of any material assistance and requires no organ of sight. By way of contrast Merleau-Ponty insists that the light of conscious illumination and reflection cannot be separated from its experience as a lived phenomenon.

Merleau-Ponty considers light as it is experienced by the seeing subject in *The Phenomenology of Perception*, where he casts the body as a synergistic unity or organizing principle underlying our sense of light. In Merleau-Ponty's later ontologically directed project, light's *de facto* existence – taken up or made meaningful in its sensible articulation – is itself the focus of interest. In conjunction with his recasting of the terms of phenomenology, Merleau-Ponty announces his turn from metaphysics in his description of an invisible co-existent within the visible or the elemental sensible flesh of an anonymous seeing. In the opening paragraph of 'The Intertwining – The Chiasm', with a desire to account for the lability of perceptual experiences at the forefront, Merleau-Ponty begins his evocation of flesh as a pre-discursive state of flux in relation to which perceptual experience is 'the insistent reminder of a mystery as familiar as it is unexplained, of a light which, illuminating the rest, remains at its source in obscurity' (1968: 130). Merleau-Ponty is referring here to a chiasmic light which has a lived reality in seeing rather than being a co-incidence or a clarification of anything. As Merleau-Ponty observes in his critique of both empiricist attempts to make perceptions into things and the intellectualist belief that perceptions can be thematized adequately in thought: 'To "live" a thing is not to coincide with it, nor fully to embrace it in thought' (1962: 325). For Merleau-Ponty light has its own synergy or organizing principle that illuminates everything in a common manner or articulates itself invisibly in every sensible thing; not by co-incidence between thought and things but carnally, in the way it is lived.

Merleau-Ponty's general approach to vision is supported by and becomes a critique of the phenomenological reformulation of light in the wake of nineteenth-century research in optics. There, the most profound change in theorizing the nature of light is the shift from emission and corpuscular optics to the wave theory of light. In the former, light is composed of rays, which emanate from a source and traverse an optical field longitudinally. The latter theory, which originates with the work of Fresnel, maintains that light is not radiant. The vibrations of light are not streams of particles but transverse interferences created by laterally propagating light waves. It has been both argued and disputed that the wave theory of light represents a paradigm shift, not only in physics, but in nineteenth-century vision generally. The most significant changes claimed for the wave theory of light are, first, that linear perspectival modes of representation no longer have a basis in optical verisimilitude and, second, the 'action at a distance' world view is drastically altered (Frankel, 1976).

However, for the purposes of this discussion, the most significant consequence of Fresnel's work is that light loses its ontological privilege. Previously the unique preserve of optics, Jonathan Crary observes that light is now equatable with the phenomena of electricity and magnetism (Crary, 1990: 88–96). Light, the noble bond which since Plato has linked together sight and visibility, inexorably begins to part company with vision and visibility. Crary traces the divergence of light into physics, once it is conceivable as electromagnetism, and the divergence of vision into the field of physiological optics, the study of the unique sensory capacities of the eye which had been first explored by Goethe and Schopenhauer. The ontological privilege of light receives its ultimate denouement in Johannes Muller's physiological studies of the senses. In relation to the sense of sight, Muller demonstrates that electrical stimulus, mechanical blows or rubbing, chemical agents and increased blood-flow are all capable of producing the sensation of light. The sensation of light has no necessary connection with any actual light. In physiological experiments light is transformed from an external agent into a sensation which resides in the capacities of a body to produce it.

In Merleau-Ponty's phenomenological reformulation of vision light is addressed as a phenomenon in a perceptual domain which is inadequately accounted for in either theoretical terms or in empirical physiological research. Merleau-Ponty begins the introduction to his first phenomenological work, *The Structure of Behaviour*, with a discussion of the distinction that is made between the so-called 'real light' of scientific understanding and 'phenomenal light' as a qualitative experience (1963: 7–10). Rather than distinguishing between these two aspects of light, Merleau-Ponty's task in this early work is to demonstrate that the nature of light dwells in the inability to objectively distinguish between the two.[1] Merleau-Ponty asserts that it is not possible to differentiate between scientific and naïve perception, because both are ultimately corporeally based. This theme is developed throughout his work. Carnal light must be distinguished from the 'natural light' of the perceiving subject that in Cartesian metaphysics is converted into the 'intelligible light' of ideas.

The value of light in Cartesian metaphysics is that it is a medium from which object-less perceptions can be formed. The light we see is not what interests the mind of reason. Our eyes are merely instruments of a mind which 'sees' a light which commands our vision from without. In Cartesian metaphysics, sensory qualities such as colour, brightness and transparency are secondary to the sense of vision, because as changeable qualities they contribute to errors of judgement about our experience of things. The light of reason is black and white (Foucault, 1970: 133). What interests Merleau-Ponty about this separation of light into essential and secondary qualities is that Descartes actually abandons the visible in order to clarify it.[2] He goes so far as to claim that Descartes virtually eliminates the necessity for visual perception by reducing vision to a sense of touch.[3] In Descartes' *Dioptrics*, the action of light is achieved by contact. The blind can see with sticks for eyes or by touching things with their hands. According to Merleau-Ponty, such action gives a supplementary status to the light of perception. Light is contracted into an unlit space, cleared of deceptive reflections, refractions and colour. Merleau-Ponty identifies these supplementary qualities of reflection, refraction and colour as the very qualities which make vision action at a distance, or give vision its scope, unlike the linear spatiality of a vision composed by touch which for Descartes gives only the *idea* of seeing. Merleau-Ponty's criticism of Descartes is not based on his inclusion of the tactile in his account of vision, but on his use of tactility to distance vision from perception. Rather than elaborating the visual domain in terms of touch or an imagined contact, Merleau-Ponty describes perception as a uniquely constituted domain in which vision and touch as well as the other senses are coextensive with each other as metonymically interrelated modes of perception.

Merleau-Ponty considers light as a phenomenon with perceptual variability. Instead of separating light and colour into primary and secondary qualities as Descartes does, he treats both as phenomenally co-existent qualities. He is also critical of contemporary objective explanations of the way we perceive colour. According to him the mistake made by empiricist and consciousness-based accounts of colour perception is the presumption that there is a true colour of a thing that remains identical in any context. The question that is posed in common by both approaches is how is it possible to know a thing's proper colour. For Merleau-Ponty the interrelatedness of lighting and colour are qualities that cannot be approached as a range of specific elements distinguishable within the perceived thing. The position that Merleau-Ponty takes is that a thing's colour cannot be abstracted from the experience of a thing, but rather 'colour in living perception is a way into the thing' (1962: 305). Our experience of a thing's colour cannot even be confined to visual experience, but has a texture that includes other perceptions of the thing, for example dimensions of tactility, sonority and smell.

This texture cannot be explained by a range of empirical variables, such as the way a thing appears in the light, the kind of light, its position in relation to other things. A belief in the prior identifiability of all these relations in perceptions is maintained by ignoring that their identification as different components of perceptional relations can occur only after the fact of perception. Merleau-Ponty argues that what perception makes explicit is that there is a synergistic unity underlying one's experience of a thing's properties. The various attributes of a thing and the background against which it is seen are internally connected in a relationship of co-existence. In perception light is taken for granted as a transparent 'lighting' or background setting of things as visual phenomena, but it can also be the object of perception, for example as a beam, as possessing a colour, or as having a particular atmosphere. The interrelatedness of lighting, colour and the dimensional relations of things in a perceptual field is not a purely objectifiable phenomenon divisible into extractable components, but involves the articulation of perceptual properties through an intentionality that is experienced by the subject as a co-existence with the phenomenon. For Merleau-Ponty, the reality of perception has no ultimately determinable basis; the more sensory articulations that are made the more real the thing is perceived to be.

Merleau-Ponty returns the seer to a world of light which is not objectifiable or inhabitable from a distance; light is objectifiable and inhabitable only from within it. Light has the diacritical structure of flesh. The ideality of light cannot be separated from the carnal experience of light. They form an intimate interlining: 'Light's transcendence is not delegated to a reading mind which deciphers the impacts of the light-thing upon the brain and which could do this quite as well if it had never lived in a body' (1964a: 178). Carnal light is not a transparent medium with its own clarity. It is the cloth or interlaced fabric of an anonymous visibility. The experience of light, as with all sensibility, comes into being, as Merleau-Ponty insists, 'within the framework of a certain setting in relation to the world which is the definition of my body' (1962: 303). This shift in its composition transforms the way light is experienced in vision.

Visual perception presupposes a mechanism that is capable of responding to light as meaningful and in different ways. In other words, it assumes a visual setting or language residing within us as a sensibility which gives us an implicit understanding of the light. This making sense of light, rather than seeing light, is the gaze.[4] It is a knowledge of light which does not come through laws of perception, but through the correspondence between the appearances of things and our kinaesthetic unfoldings as bodies in a world (1962: 310). Merleau-Ponty proposes that the seeing subject's experience of a visible world and the constitution of the visual field are not pre-existent relationships that are known by thought or rational judgement. They are discernible by a bodily orientation in respect of a situation or thing, which has the capacity to be unthinkingly incorporated as an habitual orientation. Thinking about or having our attention drawn to the corporeal basis of our knowledge of these relationships only gives an awareness that they are known without thought.

In the context of visual perception, the eye loses its instrumental relation to light. Merleau-Ponty stresses that the eye is not an instrument, but an organ. Instruments are detachable organs, not the reverse (1964a: 178). The eye's participation in vision cannot be divorced from the carnality of light; it cannot see in terms of sheer light. To see light is to see nothing else. When the eye is represented as the instrument of vision it is assumed incorrectly that the eye takes the 'lighting' of its gaze into account:

The eye is not the mind, but a material organ. How could it ever take anything 'into account?' It can do so only if we introduce the phenomenal body beside the objective one, if we make a knowing-body of it, and if, in short, we substitute for consciousness, as the subject of perception, existence, or being in the world through a body.

(Merleau-Ponty, 1962: 309n)

For Merleau-Ponty, the eye which sees things through the coincidence of light is replaced by the knowing-body as condition of lighting. Lighting is the lining of what it is that we see, the assumed intermediary directing or supporting our gaze. We do not see. We perceive in conformity with a carnal light that already knows and sees, because it is not detachable from the things we see. Lighting supports our gaze as a background of sensibility.

Lighting is an assumed light in the sense of an involvement that the body has entered into and acquired in coming into being in the world. It is a synergy that is maintained as a potentiality without a formal qualitative or substantive presence:

The lighting is neither colour nor, in itself, even light, it is anterior to the distinction between colours and luminosities. This is why it always tends to become 'neutral' for us. The penumbra in which we are becomes so natural that it is no longer even perceived as penumbra.

(Merleau-Ponty, 1962: 311)

Supported by a primordial lighting, light appears as a neutral property common to all visibles.

Merleau-Ponty gives a new inflection to the qualitative aspects of light which are elsewhere attributed with introducing errors into vision. There is a structuring which allows a variability in our sense of light: 'Lighting and the constancy of the thing illuminated, which is its correlative, are directly dependent on our bodily situation' (1962: 310). Merleau-Ponty considers the multiplicity of interrelated factors as *feats* not qualitative components of visual perception. The phenomenon of constancy refers to the constancy of light which is maintained throughout its differences. The differences of brightness we observe in light are directly related to our establishment within it. A white disc of light from a lamp becomes a light which I no longer see but which envelops me and becomes the condition of my seeing things as I move into it. Colour has a constancy as a light which adheres to things even when they change colour. A table can still remain brown when a change in light colours it differently, by my substituting the actuality of colour for the memory of colour (1962: 304). Merleau-Ponty discusses a wide variety of other empirically observed variables of light from surface effects such as glow, gloss and transparency, to the changes of light in after-images. These all reiterate the constancy of light in its multiple and changeable phenomenal dimensions.

The constancy of light is articulated within the organization of a field. Contrasts in light are directly related to the foregrounding or backgrounding effects of a field. Merleau-Ponty lists differences in the constancy of light which can be accounted for in terms of the effects of peripheral and central vision, monocular and binocular vision, coloured and uncoloured light, brief and prolonged vision. The significance of these observations is not that they prove a functional relation between the phenomenon of constancy, the articulation of a field and the phenomenon of lighting. Rather, they refer to an apparatus which underlines and conveys within its structure the nature of the visual world. Merleau-Ponty describes a similar mechanism to lighting that operates in tactile as well as other perception. The constancy of light within a field is indicative of a scope of lighting – as an aim or field of possibility which can be contrasted with a concept of light majestically traversing an abstract space.

In *The Visible and the Invisible* Merleau-Ponty reinterprets the co-existence and variability of perceptions as a function of a common sensibility rather than a unifying body-consciousness. The associative generality of an unlimited flesh is itself proposed as a synergistic unity underlining all modes of sensibility. Here lighting is the index of a common sense of being, or a reality that is transposable between bodies as sensing things:

> Why would not the synergy exist among different organisms, if it is possible within each? Their landscapes interweave, their actions and their passions fit together exactly: this is possible as soon as we no longer make belongingness to one same 'consciousness' the primordial definition of sensibility, and as soon as we rather understand it as the return of the visible upon itself, a carnal adherence of the sentient to the sensed and of the sensed to the sentient. For as overlapping and fission, identity and difference, it brings to birth a ray of natural light that illuminates all flesh and not only my own.
>
> (Merleau-Ponty, 1968: 142)

Merleau-Ponty reinvests light with a carnal significance which has been lost in its objective or metaphysical conception. Rather than a light that is realizable as thought or a consciousness of things, light's reality is co-existent with its sensible articulation. Illumination is the knowledge of a common belonging in the world, or assumption of a unifying pact accompanying all experiences. This is a knowledge which cannot be ripped from phenomena but is a sensed reality or lighting inscribing and inscribed within them.

Lighting is not light itself. Lighting is the chiasm of light, or light as flesh. Lighting belongs to the 'body', whose irreducible obscurity is an opening against which, or in whose divergent senses, there can be a coming to light of a perceivable world. Merleau-Ponty refers to this chiasmic grounding of the visible as a 'pro-vision-al partitioning' (1968: 152),[5] or a latency which divides/makes possible the passage between an interior horizon of light as sensation and an external horizon of lighted things: 'What senses = I cannot posit one sole sensible without positing it as torn from my flesh, lifted off my flesh, and my flesh itself is one of the sensibles in which an inscription of all the others is made' (1968: 259).

While reinvesting light with a carnal significance, 'lighting' is open to criticism as a 'first light' which encourages a vision of the pure intentionality of things in the world. Foucault expresses his criticism of Merleau-Ponty's faith in the chiasm's mystery, describing it as an attempt to instate empirical experience as a new transcendentalism.[6] Against the obscurity of this pure intentionality, Foucault distinguishes between the realm of language and the realm of light as two orders – those of discourse and of vision. Rather than lying within the realm of the body, the constitution and interrelation between both these realms is the proper realm of knowledge. Foucault's separation allows him to account for a history of modes of seeing based on the functioning of knowledges.[7] Hence, for example, medical knowledge is able to modulate a 'first light' in which it constituted a space of visibility for illness.[8]

However, in his hostility to phenomenal faith Foucault dismisses Merleau-Ponty's 'first light' too quickly. 'Lighting' contains within it an account of natural light as an opening on to a common (human) being (Merleau-Ponty, 1964c: 239). When Foucault refers to the constitution of the field of visibility for illness in terms of the use of, for example, 3D to restore depth to the eye and volume to pain, he demonstrates how medicine relies on the belief in a commonly held language of perception as the universal modulator of this 'first light'. A more sympathetic reading would focus on Merleau-Ponty's insistence on the fundamental historicity of a body's taking up of meaning, emphasizing the open-endedness of its texture rather than the obscure ordering of its perceptions. In Merleau-Ponty's formulation there is no such thing as a 'first light' of a fixable constitution, only the 'first light' of an historical lived 'lighting'. The 'first light' which is taken on faith in medical knowledge would be a perfect example of the mechanism by which we are corporeally inserted into a common medical world. This is a world to which we are intentionally drawn or can articulate ourselves in only in so far as we experience a unity with or self-perception in common with the object-body of medical perception. It is a faith in a world of anonymous perception where one's body is never entirely one's own but is an imminent reality that is ever on the verge of changing.[9]

A criticism of a different kind can be levelled at Merleau-Ponty's depiction of the knowing-body as the condition of lighting. The lighting of the know-ing-body carries with it an intentionality which dispassionately takes its indefinable corporeal meaning into account. Such an organ-ization of vision into what Merleau-Ponty refers to as 'one sole Cyclopean vision' (1968: 141) is a flesh that lacks any disruptive potential or the powers to override rational thought. By way of contrast, Georges Bataille's 'pineal' or 'third' eye is charged with heightened vision, which in its reflexive capacity is 'a sexual organ of unheard-of sensitivity' (Bataille, 1985: 77) capable of seeing all manner of things with a transgressive propensity unknown to reason. In Merleau-Ponty's account the sensing of the knowing body, or 'carnal adher-ence of the sentient to the sensed and the sensed to the sentient' is a 'ray of natural light that illuminates all flesh and not only my own' (1968: 142). In Bataille's account the uncontrollable couplings of carnal vision is an excre-ment which is offensive to reason. The hyper-reflex of rational vision is not a metaphysical incorporation of an ambiguous void. It is a gut reflex to void. The pineal eye spurts tears and blood as its own form of illumination. Its visions are the excessive illuminations of an improper body which, far from adhering to any intentional formation, are so grotesquely ambiguous in their shameless proliferation of coherences that they make reason shit and vomit.[10]

Both Bataille and Merleau-Ponty refer to a blind spot in the light of reason, but that blindness is represented very differently by each. For Merleau-Ponty the blind spot is the invisible corporeal underlining of all objective speculation, or flesh of which the eye is formed but cannot see itself. For Bataille, the blind spot is the effect of corporeal illumination, which rents the eye of rational vision. While Bataille's project aims at divesting speculative thinking of its authority through a reflex evacuation of the rational eye, Merleau-Ponty's knowing-body overlooks the unintentionality of the reflex actions of the eye. Merleau-Ponty discusses the phenomenon of blinking: 'With each flutter of my eyelashes a curtain lowers and rises, though I do not think for an instant of imputing this eclipse to the things themselves; with each movement of my eyes that sweep the space before me the things suffer a brief torsion, which I also ascribe to myself' (1968: 7), but he cannot account for the imperative to blink in terms of the intentionality of lighting.

Merleau-Ponty speaks of the blink as a reflex action which is related to the maintenance of a visual field rather than the aspecular dissolution of flesh into a state of flux.[11] The blink is a primordial divergence in the persistence of perception which opens up the field of vision. Vision is formed in/between a dividing membrane, a partitioning between an interior and an exterior horizon (1968: 152). But the blink is more than a momentary confrontation of vision with its own blind spot or point of the gaze losing sight of itself that divides/reopens the field of vision. Merleau-Ponty himself refers to a passive or ungazing vision which is dazzled by and unable to make sense of light. Rather than opening up a visual scope, with the loss of an identifiable orientation of the seer in relation to it, light becomes an invasive foreign body from which the eyes recoil in pain, blinking and watering senselessly on alien contact (1962: 315). Here Merleau-Ponty is describing the cessation of light as a visual phenomenon at the point where it becomes a merely physical encounter, that is, no longer a *de facto* lighting.

Merleau-Ponty speaks of the reversibility of light based on an originary 'lighting' of a body in contact with the world, but between the interior and the exterior horizon of the visible there is a field of moisture, a fluid milieu renewing itself between the touching/dividing eyelids. This is a lapse of a different nature from lighting's pro-vision-al subjective/objective divide. It is an unintentional dissolution of or tear in the field of vision. What Merleau-Ponty does not enter further into is the blink as an abandonment of vision in its very flesh or lapsing of chiasmic lighting, which would be a shedding of everything, including a being unable to recollect itself in a fluidity without scope. Even in its visual lapses Merleau-Ponty preserves the visual attitude of a body-consciousness that is, as he describes it, 'prepared for a self-perception' (1968: 9), or a reflexive preoccupation with an imaginary identity that is never entirely lost sight of.

The specular body

Merleau-Ponty bases his non-dualist formulation of subjectivity on an originary anonymous rather than reflective or intersubjective nature of vision. This is a position which undermines the Cartesian formulation of the human subject as an isolated ego who is in command of or able to view his body and its actions from a rational perspective. The body of the Cartesian subject is experienced by introspection or the capacity to reflect on one's feelings, desires and perceptions. By way of contrast, Merleau-Ponty turns the contents of consciousness outwards, into a consciousness of one's body that is experienced as a postural schema or the perception of a bodily orientation in relationship to the world. Similarly, the perception of others and the sharing of perceptual experience is possible, not because the bodies of others are recognisable as projections of one's own body, but because they have a perceivable comportment and intentionality as relationships that are translatable between bodies. As the schema within which the subject can be articulated in the world, the experience of embodiment becomes the horizon of possibility for all intersubjective and objective relations. The bodies of others are not objects; they are phenomena that are coextensive with one's own body (Merleau-Ponty, 1964a: 118).

Merleau-Ponty rereads Descartes' mind/body dualism in a more complex way in his later work, referring to it as 'perhaps the most profound idea of the union of the soul and the body' (1968: 234). Descartes earns this unexpected accolade for conceptualizing the human body as non-closed, or irreducible to a body in itself. A human body is open to conjecture in Descartes' schema because thought predetermines its existence. Unlike the closed immediacy of an animal body a body has human form only as a different form of itself. In Descartes' case the idea of a human body is achieved in a 'view of itself' or thought of itself. In Merleau-Ponty's case, the idea of a human body is experienced in a social context, that is in the view or perception of others.

Merleau-Ponty loosely adheres to the general psychoanalytic premise that the earliest stage of childhood is characterized by an undifferentiated anonymous collectivity in which the child has no sense of a distinction between itself and others.[12] The emergence of the self–other distinction is charted as a progressive experience of self-alienation in relation to the specular image of both the child and others. The divergence between the direct experience and image of others is the means by which the infant discovers the body-image as evidence of his or her own self-alienation or objectifiability.[13]

Merleau-Ponty emphasizes that the specular body is not originally 'me'. It is first an image which is 'mine', not in so far as it is a projection of mine but in so far as it is given to me from without. There are, for example, parts of my body which others, but not I, can see. The body of the perceiving subject is given form and content through its experience of surrounding objects. These surrounding objects reflect and affirm a body schema which is gradually built up

51

through this interaction; a mapping of both body and surroundings in relation to one another. The acquisition of the specular image – the image discovered in the mirror – launches the child into the visible world, capable of being seen by itself or others. In other words the body schema is not an entirely internal construct, but one which is seen from outside – in a mirror or by others.[14] As Merleau-Ponty notes in 'The Child's Relation with Others', the assumption of a specular body is far from fixed. It remains a fascination which persists throughout life. Although the child gradually acquires a sense of individuality which continues to develop throughout life, that sense is never entirely complete. Aspects of synchretic co-existence and indeterminacy persist in adult life, where others are perceived collectively as part of a common world.

In *The Visible and the Invisible* Merleau-Ponty reworks the idea of a synchretic sociability based on the translatability of a postural schema in his account of a carnal or anonymous flesh. Here the relationship between perceiver and perceived is mediated by an anonymous visibility, in which seeing is both an individual or incarnate experience and occurs in a body that is coextensive with or open to others in the visible world. It is of the essence of visual perception that in order for me to see I must be visible for an other. Visibility is by definition a relation of reversibility:

> he who sees cannot possess the visible unless he is possessed by it, unless he *is of it*, unless, by principle, according to what is required by the articulation of the look with the things, he is one of the visibles, capable by a singular reversal, of seeing them – he who is one of them.
>
> (Merleau-Ponty, 1968: 134–5)

In order for the seer to be able to see or the touching hand to touch from the 'inside' each must pass over to the 'other' side and become something that is visible or touched. To see is first and foremost to see oneself as being seen by an other. Being seen is a vulnerability which is essential to visibility, but that vulnerability, or openness to being other, comes only because as a seer I am of the visible. In other words, seeing and being seen are inextricably bound up together.

Although Merleau-Ponty does not limit the idea of a body to a visible image, the visible is paradigmatic of the reversibility and divergence which characterizes all narcissistic or egological relations. Body-image is neither an internally derived corporeal schema nor an externally derived Gestalt. It is an image which exists in negotiation between both. Together, vision and narcissism participate in defining each other in a double sense. One of these is the self-reflexive or mirror-sense of seeing 'oneself' as the subject of visual (and other) phenomena: 'since the seer is caught up in what he sees, it is still himself he sees: there is a fundamental narcissism of all vision' (1968: 139). What is being considered here is the body folded back on itself in its otherness as a seeable, feelable, audible thing. The body is the hinge which inserts the seer within the visible as an object of visual perception, or a reflexivity that prefigures what is commonly called self-consciousness.

The body folded back on itself underlies the narcissism of vision understood in a more basic sense of participating in a common visibility of which one is simultaneously constituted as a part:

> not to see in the outside, as the others see it, the contours of a body one inhabits, but especially to be seen by the outside, to exist within it, to emigrate into it, to be seduced, captivated, alienated by the phantom, so that the seer and the visible reciprocate one another and we no longer know which sees and which is seen.

> (Merleau-Ponty, 1968: 139)

The body is not a thing but that through which there is an openness that comes with being a visible for others. Its obverse and reverse dimensionality is made explicit by the presence of others. For example, this interaction can be seen in the childhood game of 'peek-a-boo', which reaches its pleasurable high point each time the hiding child 'finds' himself or herself for the other player. What delights the child is the circulation of a body made visible to both players in the reversibility of the look.[15]

The body as a sensing and sensible thing – as always other or divergent in itself – is the invisible structuring element that constitutes a common visible. This experience cannot be objectified because it is an openness on to and movement between self and other that reveals a thing as a phenomenon rather than being based on a thing. In this sense the corporeality of experience is a consciousness or 'ideal vision' of the world and things. The human body is a flesh that is capable of seeing itself in the world by seeing that world as flesh able to be reversed or seen:

> At the frontier of the mute or solipsistic world, where, in the presence of other seers, my visible is confirmed as an exemplar of a universal visibility, we reach a second or figurative meaning of vision, which will be the *intuitus mentis* or idea, a sublimation of the flesh, which will be mind or thought.

But the factual presence of other bodies could not produce thought or the idea if its seed were not in my own body.

(Merleau-Ponty, 1968: 145)

The specular image is the means of translating the visual body into a socio-psychological space (O'Neill, 1986: 206). In this sense the visible underlines one's cultural existence in a corporeally based relationship of reciprocal co-existence with others. Merleau-Ponty bases this reciprocity on the common world of perceptual faith. The common world of perceptual faith is the non-substantiable presupposition, already discussed, that we share the same anonymous lived-world, based on a pre-linguistic postural identification (Merleau-Ponty, 1968: 142). The basis of this reciprocity is gestural, a transitivity no different from an infant's responding with a smile to another smiling face. It is elicited by and elicits a posturally based, rather than calculated correspondence of bodily conduct. This anonymous sensibility is never lost. It persists as the expectation of mutual recognition which is, according to Merleau-Ponty, the condition of all egological and social inter-actions in adult life.

Because the infant responds to the mirror image as an image, it makes a distinction between the specular or objectifiable body and its subjective self. The specular body is the point at which an anonymous seeing turns to visible flesh:

through a labor upon itself the visible body provides for the hollow whence a vision will come, inaugurates the long maturation at whose term suddenly it will see, that is, will be visible for itself, will institute the interminable gravitation, the indefatigable metamorphosis of the seeing and the visible whose principle is posed and which gets underway with the first vision.

(Merleau-Ponty, 1968: 147)

The first vision is 'seeing', or the visibility of the look to itself (a re-pli-cation of visibility supported by the look of others). As Lefort emphasizes, the gaze is detachable from the subject (1990: 7). It can turn around, as in the case of Freud's 'wolf-man', and come back as though it came from the thing seen. The replication of the synchretic origin of visual perception is the key to the meaning of terror (a child is terrified by his own look which he sees reversed in the eyes of the wolves).[16]

There is a significant difference between Merleau-Ponty's and Jean-Paul Sartre's formulation of the seer's vulnerability to the other's look. Like Merleau-Ponty, Sartre insists that recognition is not a self-contained act of conscious reflection, but unlike Merleau-Ponty he theorizes his account of the gaze solely from the perspective of the subject. In Sartre's post-Hegelian account of human consciousness self-recognition is essentially intersubjective in nature in so far as it is occasioned by the challenge presented to the self made the object of an other's gaze. At issue for Sartre is the freedom to define oneself through one's own action and free choice in the face of an unavoidable opposing consciousness, or an other's self-interested objectifying point of view. By way of contrast, Merleau-Ponty stresses the impossibility of seeing the other as an opposing point of view. Instead, for Merleau-Ponty, as a seer I borrow my ego from others, and from their bodily comportment I represent them as sharing visual experiences in common with me. Rather than the other's gaze contesting my own, in order for me to see at all I must be visible for an other. My gaze is a capacity for making sense of light or a perceptual field that gives meaning to what I see in the dehiscence between seeing and being seen by the other. Sartre describes my being in the world which is revealed to me by the gaze of the other as an alienating experience in which my freedom is contested by another individual's perspective. By way of contrast Merleau-Ponty's synchretic account of the gaze offers a mechanism for explaining how an individual can have experiences that are perceived in a collective immediacy with others and share a world, a culture and a social life with them.

Jacques Lacan's account of the gaze is closer to Merleau-Ponty's in so far as Lacan argues that the viewing subject is not simply the point of convergence of light from an object (which is the basis of geometrical perspective or a vision that maps space but not visual perception). The scopic field is represented by Lacan in a double dihedral (Lacan, 1979: 106). The seeing subject is itself the effect of the relationship that it has with its object, seen (in the sense of being mapped) from the perspective of a light which emanates from that point. The institution of the subject in the visible is dependent on the seer being 'photographed' (1979: 106), or inscribed from the outside by a gaze that structures or determines the way it makes sense of light. However, Lacan's account of the gaze differs in a significant way from Merleau-Ponty's. There is a dehiscence in the visual field between what is looked at and what is seen. This schism dispossesses the subject of the gaze while giving the seer a sense of being within it. As a self that is elsewhere or always other to itself the subject of the gaze is attempting to make up for an unapprehensible lack. The subject is able to see its look only by giving it up to an externally mediated order of constitution or symbolic substitute.

An important feature of Merleau-Ponty's analysis of the dehiscence between seer and specular body is that it is not confined to the visible. Seeing is a reflexivity of the body which is experienced by means of touch. While Merleau-Ponty discusses vision and touch in 'The Intertwining – The Chiasm' as though the two senses are metonymically equivalent, he expresses the dehiscence between seeing and visibility by means of the analogy of the two hands touching. He claims an equivalence between the stereopsis of the visible and the double touching of the tangible: 'because there exists a very peculiar relation from one to the other, across the corporeal space – like that holding between my two eyes – making of my hands one sole organ of experience' (1968: 141).

The point which Merleau-Ponty is making is that the senses participate in inaugurating multiple experiences of a body as a sensibly constituted unity. However, it is the double touching initially which conveys the chiasm in/between which that unity is interposed: '. . . if these experiences never exactly overlap, if they slip away at the very moment they are about to rejoin, if there is always a "shift," a "spread," between them, this is precisely because my two hands are part of the same body' (1968: 148). The unique contribution of the double touching is that in its reversibility it is a contact with the other which is always imminent, but never realized. Unlike the distance separating the seer from the specular body which is required for mirror reflection, the spacing of the two hands touching conveys a sense of unity in the folding back upon itself of the *same* body.

In Merleau-Ponty's schema of tactility the body is sensed as both an auto-affective structure and as a pure negative, or outside. He brings the two senses of embodiment together in/between the two hands by describing the two hands touching in terms of the body mirroring itself. As Derrida argues, a body touching/being-touched is not primarily an auto-affective structure because 'the surface of my body, as something external, must begin by being exposed in the world' (Derrida, 1973: 79). Only after the insertion of a mirror do the hands become autoaffective organs. The experience of self-reflexive unity is specific to the hands, which Merleau-Ponty makes paradigmatic of the tactility of the rest of a body. However, not all tactile surfaces of the body can be felt as both self and other self-reflexively, and the mucous membranes of the eyelids, lips and labia can touch each other together but cannot be differentiated as a body feeling or being felt, that is, a body reversible at will.

Each time Merleau-Ponty refers to the reversibility of the visible, he includes touch with vision, reinforcing reversibility as a combination of touch-vision:

the flesh we are speaking of is not matter. It is the coiling over of the visible upon the seeing body, of the tangible upon the touching body, which is attested to in particular when the body sees itself, touches itself seeing and touching the things, such that, simultaneously, *as* tangible it descends among them, *as* touching it dominates them all and draws this relationship and even this double relationship from itself, by dehiscence or fission of its own mass . . . these two mirror arrangements of the seeing and the visible, the touching and the touched, form a close-bound system that I count on, define a vision in general and a constant style of visibility from which I cannot detach myself, even when a particular vision turns out to be illusory.

(Merleau-Ponty, 1968: 146)

When Merleau-Ponty discusses the intertwining of the visible and tangible, emphasis falls on touch and vision as senses functioning organically in common; both vision and touch, and indeed all the senses are a flesh of organic mirrors. What this correspondence allows is an elision of the body-of-the-hands which can be reversed at will and the reversibility of the specular body. In other words, the reflexivity of 'first vision' or the flesh of seeing rests on a body which, by virtue of its being able to feel itself in its dehiscence, can see itself in the difference between seeing and being seen.

Merleau-Ponty's interpretation of the tangible body gives an intentional inflection to the reversibility of the look, but that is not how it is always experienced. Approaching the problem from the side of bodily existence, Iris Marion Young's analysis of pregnant embodiment, for example, challenges the conceptualization of the body's experience of itself in dualist terms of subject and object. In pregnancy, the 'intentional arc' that unifies experience bodily is in flux. The pregnant subject is other to herself in a way which defies Merleau-Ponty's understanding of the self as always other to itself. Young argues that in pregnancy the body is neither subject nor object; rather it is neither limited to nor different from its material being (Young, 1985).

In her work on various aspects of feminine body comportment Young adheres more closely than Merleau-Ponty to his own existential phenomenology by stressing the situated nature of experience. Visual experience is not separable from the informative orientation of the postural schema in a historico-cultural milieu. Young cites the example of women's objectification, but the example can extend to the objectifiability of any body depending on the context in which the body is seen, be that a medical context, a sexual context

57

or a workplace. That objectifiability is 'the ever-present possibility that one will be gazed upon as a mere body, as shape and flesh that presents itself as the potential object of another subject's intentions and manipulations, rather than as a living manifestation of action and intention' (Young, 1990: 55). Young's criticism of Merleau-Ponty's continuation of the subject and object dichotomy in his existential phenomenology echoes Merleau-Ponty's own motive for his ontological reworking of phenomenology as flesh. However, the same dichotomous view of the body is preserved indirectly in his account of the tangible as flesh. A body's vulnerability in its aspect for an other as an object in perception is of a different order to that vulnerability being felt as exposure to the possibility of bodily interference. This is the experience of intentionality being stripped away or the tangible reduction to a no-body.

The limits of specularity, which Merleau-Ponty both reveals and is revealed as supplementing in his phenomenological reworking, have been the subject of a variety of poststructuralist critiques. Rodolphe Gasché's critique of specular identity is among the best known of these. Based on Derrida's deconstruction of the metaphysics of presence, Gasché's analysis lays emphasis on the inappropriateness of associating reflection with the unity of consciousness and knowledge:

> The alterity that splits reflection from itself and thus makes it able to fold itself into itself – to reflect itself – is also what makes it, for structural reasons, incapable of closing upon itself. The very possibility of reflexivity is also the subversion of its own source. . . . It opens itself to the thought of an alterity, a difference that remains unaccounted for by the polar opposition of source and reflection, principle and what is derived from it, the one and the Other.
>
> (Gasché, 1986: 102)

Gasché highlights the *différance* or irreducible otherness which defers the possibility of specular identity. Vision, in its reflexivity, is the sense which attempts to represent the unrepresentable, and necessarily fails in the act. Described in these terms the specular is the economy in which the subject gives birth to itself within the traces of its dispersal. The consequences for an identity based on self-reflection is a sense of loss accompanying the universal investiture of the specular.

'With the first vision, the first contact, the first pleasure', Merleau-Ponty says, 'there is initiation, that is, not the positing of a content, but the opening of a dimension that can never be closed' (1968: 151). This opening is a hollow, 'a certain absence, a negativity that is not nothing' (1968: 151). It is a carnal meaning or invisible which is encrypted within the flesh of the visible. Merleau-Ponty draws this negativity which is not nothing in terms of an abbreviated schema of touch based on mirror reflection. In his account of carnality, the body is always other or di-visible in the same way in vision and touch.

5

Touching Flesh

The body as given

For Merleau-Ponty the sensible body, not a mind capable of rational thought, is the reserve of a common human understanding. 'Massive' flesh is a pre-subjective, elemental corporeality of which the world is made before 'I' am there. This anonymous flesh 'innate to Myself' is not matter, or mind, or substance of any kind (1968: 139). It is an 'other subject', or a bodily mode in tangible proximity with thought, touching upon but not identical with self-consciousness:

> since it cannot be oriented 'in itself,' my first perception and my first hold upon the world must appear to me as action in accordance with an earlier agreement reached between x and the world in general, my history must be the continuation of a prehistory and must utilize the latter's required results. My personal existence must be the resumption of a prepersonal tradition. There is, therefore, another subject beneath me, for whom a world exists before I am here, and who marks out my place in it. This captive or natural spirit is my body, not that momentary body which is the instrument of my personal choices and which fastens upon this or that world, but the system of anonymous 'functions' which draw every particular focus into a general project.
>
> (Merleau-Ponty, 1962: 254)

Merleau-Ponty proposes the sensible body as the fund of the manner in which the world is always already there for me, unaccountably incorporating me in its generality. The conceivability of being-other-to-itself, that is, of reflective judgements and subjective relations, is born of the idealization or folding back on itself of an anonymous carnality. The body is a locus of sensing that is pre-discursively given: 'The central phenomenon, at the root of my subjectivity and my transcendence towards others, consists in my being given to myself. *I am given*, that is, I find myself already situated and involved in a physical and social world' (1962: 360).

For Merleau-Ponty subjectivity is an effect of the disparity between consciousness and the 'being in the world' of massive flesh. Consciousness is not reducible to the sensible body, and, as such, obliges the subject to an anonymous other (a carnal being) as the source of its givenness. Nor is the subject separable from flesh as the mysterious generator of that which appears as universal, mutual knowledge to the world of consciousness. The subject is not reducible to what it experiences and is equally unable to withdraw itself from anything that it experiences. Subjectivity is a freedom that is experienced in the chiasmic relation that it has in its situation in the world: '*I am given to myself*, which means that this situation is never hidden from me, it is never round me as an alien necessity, and I am never in effect enclosed in it like an object in a box' (1962: 360). Subjectivity is a vision and knowledge that comes of flesh – a coincidence of being born into a world.

The inconceivable fund of massive flesh which is always already given in reflection is given to consciousness, not as a private thing of which it is an agent, but as a gift. The anonymous sensing being which is innate but not reducible to myself as a living human being has an exposition which is anterior to the present and, as such, cannot be formally represented (Taylor, 1987: 79–81). As gift, the carnal body defies apprehension as an object of knowledge. Merleau-Ponty emphasizes that it is not possible to establish the facticity of the body which is given as gift. This formulation of subjectivity presents a problem in Merleau-Ponty's work because without facticity the pre-discursive body cannot legitimate an account of the nature of existence. That I am given to myself is not something that can be so simply claimed. As Derrida states: 'For there to be gift, it is necessary that the gift not even appear, that is not be perceived or received as gift' (1992: 173).

The gift, as both Derrida and Merleau-Ponty in his later work conceive of it, is the problem of pre-discursive identity. Merleau-Ponty elaborates the carnal body as a pre-discursive structure in the reversibility of touch. Touch for Merleau-Ponty is the sense in which the body authorizes itself, is given to itself pre-symbolically, where sensible being has a tangibility for consciousness that is not related to a factual body or the body as a pre-existent thing. Merleau-Ponty appeals to a pre-discursive bodily mode of existence in the innate proximity, never to be realized, of that which is given to itself reflexively in the double-touch.

Merleau-Ponty's idea of the body as the reserve of a common human understanding is partly informed by Marcel Mauss's theorizing of the gift as the foundation of social exchange (Mauss, 1969).[1] Derrida criticizes Mauss's theory on the basis that he presents the gift as the condition of economic exchange, where equality of identity is assumed (Derrida, 1992). In Derrida's reading of Mauss's work the gift underlies the artifice of this equivalence by constituting the social identity of individuals in relation to one another. Prestige is bestowed on the recipient, together with a moral obligation to maintain a social bond which reflects the generosity and hence status of the giver. In being given, the gift strikes its bond by impelling the return to its origin. Mauss interprets this return in terms of the cyclical pressure of consumption, nourishment and satiation. In other words, the gift is the inauguration of a systematic incorporation. The power of the gift is derived from its remaining perpetually a part of the identity of the giver, establishing a form of circulation that is imposed by the obligation to return to its origin, the place from which it is given. On Mauss's model, the gift is effectively returnable, acknowledged for example by men materially observing their obligation to their wives and to the families of the wives given to them as gifts.

For Derrida, the gift refers to an apprehended imperative or credit accorded to the other which defies comprehension as an object of knowledge. In order for there to be gift, some 'one' has to give some 'thing' to some 'one other'. Giving would be meaningless without these terms. At the same time, there can be no recognition of this giving. Any recognition of gift would annul it by casting it in terms of return, or symbolic equivalence. To recognize or name the gift as gift would be to constitute it in the economy of exchange, thereby simultaneously establishing its facticity in terms of equivalence and annulling it as gift. Derrida examines the gift as the very figure of the impossible, the very element of invisibility.[2] Mauss's analysis of the gift is caught in the contradictory insistence that there is no gift without the bind of obligation, and yet unless the gift is free of contractual obligation it is not a gift. The impossibility of gift is the impossibly dispersed structure of identity, which cannot be claimed without entering into reckoning and debt. The gift has a unique relation to the visible; it presents itself in so far as it absents itself from the economy of being seen, or the common light of day. The given in the gift is a withdrawal from the proper. The difficulty which Derrida's analysis throws up here is the naming of that withdrawal as anonymous being. According to Derrida, both donor and recipient of the gift are already given credit as such in Mauss's model, thereby pre-empting and destroying the possibility of the gift.

The impossibility of gift for Derrida is the impossibility of a difference beyond oppositional equivalence. The giving of gift means the inauguration of a relationship which takes nothing into account. It would be nothing but the inauguration of difference, and would have to come into being nondiscursively. Such difference would have to be incalculable and yet creditable, or impossible but given in that which is present. The gift is Derrida's way of evoking the passage between binary difference and difference as otherness that cannot be thought. However, the problem as Derrida puts it is that this gift is a gap in being or a being 'without being (it)' (1992: 183). While Merleau-Ponty refers to a pre-discursive nameless 'empirical pregnancy' of which subjectivity is reflexively born, Derrida announces the challenge of the pre-discursive as the structure of gift. Rather than a being in the world that is anonymously given, the origin of the given becomes the 'aporetic paralysis' of a giving whose forgetting by donor and recipient must be so radical that it never even engages in the structure of remembering (to which it could return as to a debt or sacrifice) (1992: 183).

Derrida approaches this aporia by acknowledging the necessity of 'rendering an account' of the gift's impossibility, that is of allowing that:

> Perhaps there is nomination, language, thought, desire, or intention only there where there is movement still for thinking, desiring, naming that which gives itself neither to be known, experienced, nor lived – in the sense in which presence, existence, determination regulate the economy of knowing, experiencing and living.
>
> (Derrida, 1992: 184)

Furthermore, Derrida refers to the rendering of an account of the desire to render an account. This is the desire to place the gift within the resources and limits of the need to answer for a gift that cannot be remembered but cannot be ignored. In other words, the gift insists on the rendering of an account of the ways in which gift is annulled in the economy of reciprocity and exchange. Derrida's analysis locates the ambivalence of the gift between the demand for an economically renderable account and the demand of a missing account. His concern is to divide the gift and thus disrupt the economic appropriation of its mythology.

While Derrida's reading of gift recasts the givenness of the self in terms of an aporia, it passes over another question which must be asked rather than settling on the question of gift. It is not an account of the gift which is called for, but an account of *who* desires to render such an elliptical account, to mythologize and obscure the imperative of gift to the point where it becomes a mystical experience. The many different ways that gift has been addressed philosophically merely serve to reiterate this inquiry. As Maurice Blanchot asks, conceding in advance that there can be no fitting answer: 'Why is the necessity of the gift so regularly expressed in our time, and yet assigned such different significance by thinkers as adverse and diverse as George Bataille, Emmanuel Levinas, Heidegger?' (Blanchot, 1986: 108–9). It is the question of who desires to render such an account at all that Irigaray engages in more directly in her reading of Merleau-Ponty's discussion of vision and touch in *The Visible and the Invisible*.

The tangible invisible

Merleau-Ponty locates the origin of intersubjective relations in a common anonymous flesh or sensible being. The double touch conveys the relation between self and other as dual elements of a singular intercorporeality or a social life that comes of a mutual knowledge of belonging to the world. I represent others as having experiences in the same way as I do, in the same way that I myself am visible from the outside as an object that others see. I imply others' interiority in borrowing my body from them, and they do likewise in extension with me.

Merleau-Ponty establishes a corporeally based correspondence between the egological relation and a common sociality by the literal extension of the touching hands in the mutual reversibility of the touching and touched in the handshake. However, rather than being a means of replicating the presupposition of the sameness of the nature of experience, Levinas stresses that there is an element of the gift in the handshake. Levinas contends that there is a fundamental difference between a sociality born of knowledge and the novelty of intercorporeality:

> the unique other who precisely is other in relation to all and any generality, is bound to me socially. That person cannot be represented and given to knowledge in his or her uniqueness, because there is no science but that of generality. . . . It is, in proximity, all the novelty of the social; proximity to the other, who eluding possession, falls to my responsibility.
>
> (Levinas, 1990a: 66)

64

Levinas makes a distinction between the uniqueness of the other whom I acknowledge as my responsibility and the other whose interiority is implied by me. Rather than a co-incidence of two elements in a mutual knowledge, the unique indifference to calculated exchange tendered in the handshake is annulled by its representation in the circuit of reciprocity. The handshake signifies a singularity which cannot be given with intention, it is the givenness of affection or the event of being affected. The handshake is an unconditional being given over to the other, which comes to pass without knowledge of it. It is an always already past, an inaugural affection. The handshake is merely the trace of this given, affection.

Levinas's account of the relationship between corporeality and sociality differs from the 'common flux of intentionalities', as Lyotard describes Merleau-Ponty's phenomenological account of an underlying originary sociability (Lyotard, 1991: 103). Levinas takes issue with a common corporeality, which is implied self-reflexively by the hands of the same body. The handshake is between the hands of different bodies. The handshake belongs to an order of sociality which is a radical separation expressed in the hand one shakes which is *not* one's own: 'One may especially wonder, then, whether such a "relation," the ethical relation, is not imposed across a *radical separation* between the two hands, which precisely do not belong to the same body, nor to a hypothetical or only metaphorical intercorporeality' (Levinas, 1990b: 59).

Levinas calls this relationship the 'non-in-difference' or strangeness of humans to one another (1990b: 60). Against Merleau-Ponty's language of sensible being, Levinas puts the origin of sensibility before history, before the order of representation (1990a: 66). Levinas transforms the visual into the sense par excellence of the supreme precariousness of investing in the circuit of a common sensibility, identifying that at the same time as Merleau-Ponty discusses the genesis of the represented other for me he presupposes the non-in-different constitution of intersubjectivity, that is, an intersubjectivity sustained by an unaccountable affection. In other words, before it is flesh representing itself as other to itself, the tangible is already the non-in-difference to touch. For Levinas, the tangible and the visible are thus sensibilities of entirely different orders of sociality.

While Levinas concentrates on the non-exchangeability of one hand for the other in the handshake, Irigaray argues that in deference to the prerequisite of visibility, or an objective existence for the seer, Merleau-Ponty divides the tangible body between the realms of subject and object. To touch oneself is the division that begins to set up the subject–predicate, subject–object distinction

(Irigaray, 1991a: 91). Irigaray contests this division in an alternative account of the two hands touching:

> Is it still 'valid,' if the *two hands* are *joined*? Which brings about something very particular in the relation feeling-felt. With no object or subject. With no passive or active, or even middle passive. A sort of fourth mode? Neither active, nor passive, nor middle passive. Always more passive than the passive. And nevertheless active. The hands joined, palms together, fingers outstretched, constitute a very particular touching. A gesture often reserved for women (at least in the West) and which evokes, doubles, the *touching of the lips* silently applied upon one another. A touching more intimate than that of one hand taking hold of the other. A phenomenology of the passage between interior and exterior. A phenomenon that remains in the interior, does not appear in the light of day, speaks of itself only in gestures, remains always on the edge of speech, gathering the edges without sealing them.
>
> (Irigaray, 1993a: 161)

Against Merleau-Ponty's preoccupation with an agent for whom perception is a holding on to things as objectives and thus a means of maintaining oneself in the world, Irigaray invokes an indeterminately maintained interiority. As Lingis states of Merleau-Ponty's perceptually based ontology: 'perception *has to* perceive things, coherent and consistent beings' (Lingis, 1991: 92). While one hand attempts to grasp the other in Merleau-Ponty's double-touch, Irigaray's contiguous touching refers to a mode of sensibility which, in maintaining itself as sensible, parts company with things.

Irigaray's formulation of the tangible body evokes a touching which defies the implication of reversibility, or the perception of things:

> Neither my hand nor the world is a 'glove,' nor can either be reduced to its clothing. Neither my hand nor the world is thus reversible. They are not pure actual phenomena, pure pellicles that are graspable one by the other, even empathetically. They have their roots, which are not reducible to the visible moment.
>
> (Irigaray, 1993a: 160)

What Irigaray notes about Merleau-Ponty's account of flesh is that he chooses the touching of two lips as a figure to express the intimacy between the reversibility of seer and visible: 'The body unites us directly with things through its own ontogenesis, by welding to one another the two outlines of which it is made, its two lips' (Merleau-Ponty, 1968: 136).[3] On Irigaray's reading, Merleau-Ponty's choice of the 'two lips' is consistent with his general appropriation of the morphology of the tactile. The lips of which Merleau-Ponty speaks are divided between the sensible body and the idealized body of the seer. These lips do not, however, belong to the same sensible, which would be the case if they are a body's lips (Irigaray, 1993a: 166).

Merleau-Ponty describes a body which can see itself touching itself and touch itself seeing itself. By way of contrast, Irigaray argues that 'two lips' express a tangible intimacy which is experienced without reference to the visible. This is not a pro-vision-al partitioning of flesh, but an interiorly constituted dimension of a different order. Refractory to the distinction between visible and invisible, the tangible invisible describes the body as a subjectless, objectless difference in the flesh; a constitution that, remaining in the interior, is never experienced as either an idea or a thing. The tangible invisible is the body as a positive reserve, a vitally constituted dimension, an adherence to indetermination rather than the surfacing of an unpresentable interior.

The tangible invisible curtails Merleau-Ponty's intertwining of the visible and the tangible, in which the look, while not superposable, would be a variant of touch. First, Irigaray argues, the look cannot take up the tangible, because the tangible body is not constituted in terms of the visible. Second, the visible is reliant on touch, but the reverse is not the case. Tactility is the primordial sense in which the body's interiority is constituted. Irigaray observes that consciousness is not possible without the sense of touch, which organizes a dwelling-place or interiority for consciousness. I would add that this observation is an ancient one. Aristotle also called touch the most basic sense of animate being.[4] Before the intentionality of the 'double touch' (which divides touch between sentient being and the touched object), the indeterminacy of the 'hands that touch without taking hold – like the lips' (Irigaray, 1993a: 170) constitutes the body as threshold or passage, neither an interior nor an exterior world.

Irigaray calls this intimate and imperceivable join of flesh the *mucous*, that is: 'that most intimate interior of my flesh, neither the touch of the outside of the skin of my fingers nor the perception of the inside of these same fingers, but another threshold of the passage . . . between' (1993a: 170). The mucous is an interior which could not be more intimately me, yet which evades my mastery.[5] The body's interiority is ungraspable in so far as it is unopposable to any other thing, and is refractory to concepts of containment and dissipation, penetration and recollection, visibility and form. To describe the indeterminacy of the mucous as unrepresentable would be to miss the point. The mucous is a continuation of the body beyond its existence as a phenomenon or an indistinguishable contiguity and porosity of interiority and skin.

What Irigaray finds valuable in Merleau-Ponty's account of vision is the extent to which it incorporates the tactile, even without being aware of the significance of the inclusion: 'His analysis of vision becomes even more detailed, more beautiful, as it accords him the privilege over the other senses, as it takes back a great deal of the phenomenology of the tactile' (1993a: 175). While critical of Merleau-Ponty's subordination of the tactile to the economy of the visual, Irigaray argues that it is precisely because he incorporates the tactile into the visual that Merleau-Ponty is able to privilege the visual. Irigaray reads 'The Intertwining – The Chiasm' as an intricate exercise in substitution. The contacts between the threads of the visual are replaced by the labyrinthine reversibility of the chiasm. Disavowing this exercise, Merleau-Ponty claims that the specular and the carnal belong to both the same and to different orders. The question which Irigaray asks instead is: 'How do they articulate with each other, exclude each other?' (1993a: 169).

Irigaray identifies the most graphic example of Merleau-Ponty's reliance on the tactile in his discussion of colour. In general, because of its relational rather than fixed qualities, colour has been assigned a supplementary role in the history of photology.[6] In contrast, Merleau-Ponty takes up colour as the very thing that 'imposes my vision upon me as a continuation of its own sovereign existence' (1968: 131). Colour is a constancy modulated within a constellation of differences, confronting me with a lability in the expression of the visible:

> a naked color, and in general a visible, is not a chunk of absolutely hard, indivisible being, offered all naked to a vision which could be only total or null, but is rather a sort of straits between exterior horizons and interior horizons ever gaping open, something that comes to touch lightly and makes diverse regions of the colored or visible world resound at the distances, a certain differentiation, an ephemeral modulation of this world – less a color or a thing, therefore, than a difference between things, and colors, a momentary crystallization of colored being or of visibility.
>
> (Merleau-Ponty, 1968: 132)

In Irigaray's estimation, Merleau-Ponty's willingness to be seduced by colour is born of its resuscitation of a carnal undertaking prior to anything of which he can distinguish himself as being a part. For Irigaray, this carnal dimension is invisible in so far as it is that which 'far from being able to yield to my decisions, obliges me to see' (1993a: 156). Colour is not constituted in any subjective sense, but in the unaccountable undertaking to see: 'Red, any color, is more in the mode of *participation* than of the solitary emergence of the concept' (1993a: 158). Rather than colour being an affect given in perception, before perception, affection is a capacity for seeing to which I have never agreed.

Despite Merleau-Ponty's preliminary sensitivity to the 'difference between things and colors' (1968: 132), Irigaray notes that he moves from an appreciation of the latency of the carnal body to its description as an organizing medium or pre-existent thing. As reversible flesh, the medium becomes a place of emergence or 'pre-possession', which supports the division of subject and things. The medium is simply neutral ground that makes possible the alternation between subject and object, visible and tangible: 'Indefinitely, he has exchanged seer and visible, touching and tangible, "subject" and "things" in an alternation, a fluctuation that would take place in a milieu that makes possible their passage from one or the other "side"' (Irigaray, 1993a: 159). The result is a phenomenology of touch that lends itself to the subjective–objective differentiation of vision.

For Merleau-Ponty, light appears not as a transcendent ideality, but is an ideality that is inextricable from its unrepresentable carnal meaning. The body's participation as a living reference in the sensing of meaning surfaces as a 'mystery, as familiar as it is unexplained, of a light which, illuminating the rest, remains at its source in obscurity' (1968: 130). By way of contrast Irigaray states: 'I see only by the touch of light' (1993a: 16). This is light which, before it is accountable in terms of the look of the seer, has a tangibility that conducts me without knowledge to the no-thing-ness of my carnality. My eyes, no less than the lighting of my gaze, are situated in what Irigaray refers to as this 'living crypt of my body' (1993a: 165). The double-touching without grasping refers also to vision:

> It can also be performed with the gaze: the eyes meet in a sort of silence of vision, a screen of resting before and after seeing, a reserve for new landscapes, new lights, a punctuation in which the eyes reconstitute for themselves the frame, the screen, the horizon of a vision.
>
> (Irigaray, 1993a: 161)

Irigaray's point suggests a reconsideration of the significance of blinking as an involuntary action upon which vision depends. Merleau-Ponty refers to the blink as a primordial divergence in the persistence of perception, which opens up the field of perception. He refers to a torsion in the light corresponding to the reversibility of the seer and the visible. In other words, Merleau-Ponty associates the blink with the eye's intentional grasp: 'with each movement of my eyes that sweep the space before me the things suffer a brief torsion, which I also ascribe to myself' (1968: 7).[7] However, the necessity of the blink for vision is bound to the necessity of the renewal of its tissue. This is not a tissue that has other sides or loses sight of itself because it is unable to see itself. The blink maintains the eye as mucous, as a latency which, while not of the visible, resuscitates the eye as a body passage, or a reserve in which another vision can begin.

For Merleau-Ponty, the visible is organized around the reversibility of the look of the seer. Seer and the visible 'reciprocate one another and we no longer know which sees and which is seen' (1968: 139). Irigaray interprets the solipsism of this self-enfolding as an attempt to re-create a sensible immediacy that has never existed. She argues that the association between the intimacy of the visible and a nostalgic view of intra-uterine life in Merleau-Ponty's first description of flesh is striking:

> he uses 'images' of the sea and the strand. Of immersion and emergence? And he speaks of the risk of the disappearance of the seer and the visible. Which corresponds doubly to a reality in intra-uterine nesting: one who is still in this night does not see and remains without a visible (as far as we know); but the other seer cannot see him. The other does not see him, he is not visible for the other, who nevertheless sees the world, but without him. And if everything, the totality, is organized around him, then the other, one could almost say, sees nothing? A disorganized world? If the mother, or the woman, only sees the world from the perspective of the maternal function, she sees nothing.
>
> (Irigaray, 1993a: 152)

Irigaray notes two invisibles operating here. First, there is the inability to be seen, which corresponds to the disappearance of the seer. Second, there is the darkness corresponding to flesh, or a maternal vision, which counts for nothing since it does not incorporate the seer. Irigaray's point is that, in the seer's attempt to re-create an imaginary intra-uterine dwelling within the economy of the visible, the tangible is cast in terms of what Irigaray calls a 'look forever organized, or disorganized, around the impossibility of seeing' (1993a: 153).

Against this depiction, Irigaray insists that the indetermination of the tangible body is not a loss of vision, but a difference which cannot be incorporated in the reversibility of the visual: '*the tangible is, and remains primary in its opening.*

Its touching on, of, and by means of the other. The dereliction of its ever touching this first touching' (1993a: 162). Irigaray reads Merleau-Ponty's unpresentable invisible as a nostalgia for an irretrievable pre-natal naïve vision. Irigaray argues that what is irretrievable in vision is not lost to touch. The fear of vanishing in a fluid milieu is the preoccupation of a body that sees 'only because it is a part of the visible in which it opens forth' (Merleau-Ponty, 1968: 153–4). For Irigaray the tangible is a mode of carnal participation that is not related to any self or other. The non-substitutibility of bodies, or 'That in which their differences consist' (Irigaray, 1993a: 167), is experienced in the divergence of touch, but this divergence cannot be recovered in the reversal between seer and visible. Nothing equivalent fulfils/takes the place of the invisibility of touch:

> The look cannot take up the tangible. Thus I never see that *in which* I touch or am touched. What is at play in the caress does not see itself. The in-between, the middle, the *medium* of the caress does not see itself. In the same way and differently, I do not see that which allows me to see, that which touches me with light and air so that I see some 'thing.'
>
> (Irigaray, 1993a: 161–2)

Irigaray questions Merleau-Ponty's description of the visible as a mode of inhabitation. In her reading of 'The Intertwining – The Chiasm' this inhabitation is achieved by re-creating an imaginary solipsistic 'intra-uterine' universe whose existence is determined by the seer's own incorporation in it:

> Enveloping things with his look, the seer would give birth to them, and/yet the mystery of his own birth would subsist in them. For now they contain this mystery of the prenatal night where he was palpated without seeing. A passive forever lacking an active. More passive than any passivity taken in a passive-active couple. A passivity that tries to turn itself into activity by sculpting, moving the totality of the world into a reversion of the intra-uterine abode.
>
> (Irigaray, 1993a: 154)

The illusion of an envelopment in a world replaces a maternity which is a mystery without the seer. Instead of leaving an opening for a phenomenology of touching without seeing, Merleau-Ponty closes the circuit of this mystery, using the fantasy of an invisible other (flesh) that foresees me to 'turn the world back on itself and return to myself after having passed to the other side' (Irigaray, 1993a: 183). Weaving back and forth, the world becomes a texture in which the subject sees both from inside and from inside-out.

71

Irigaray maintains that in the elision of the carnal and the maternal the maternal is absorbed to the circuit of the one ontological tissue which gives birth to itself (1993a: 154). Merleau-Ponty's elision can be contrasted to Derrida's reference to the ontological priority of the maternal, alive endlessly, encrypted, forever/never there (Derrida, 1986: 117).[8] Even in attributing his birth to woman, the son cannot acknowledge her. In remembering her she stands apart from him, as irreducible to an object of his own memory. He has no memory of his mother. The memory is his introjection. The maternal keeps open the question of sexual difference in terms of an other of whom the son has no memory but through whom he addresses himself: 'I call my mother in myself, recall myself to my mother' (1986: 117).

Irigaray describes the tangible invisible as a renewable carnality rather than a carnality that cannot come to light. The longing which Merleau-Ponty projects into the desired prediscursive inter-world is for an invisible in which the reversibility of seeing and being seen is given. For Irigaray the tangible invisible is a non-reflexive indetermination of flesh in/between flesh. The tangible invisible is a body reserve which is not subject or object and not active or passive. It is an attentiveness devoid of anticipation or resistance. Rather than questioning the ontological status of a mode of being in the world that is implicated with the gift or a body that is given in an interval of non-return, there is according to Irigaray no question of a return within touch to a pre-possessable other being.

Part III

PERVERSE LIGHT

6

Introduction to Levinas

While Merleau-Ponty's philosophy can be characterized as a philosophy of ambiguity, Levinas pursues the theme of anarchy or, more specifically, *an-archē* in his work. Merleau-Ponty demonstrates the fundamental indeterminacy of self and other in perception. Levinas makes a critical distinction between phenomenological experience, for which vision remains his paradigm, and an ethical respons(e)ibility towards an incommensurably different other. Levinas claims that there is difference which persists without the weight or force of any formal structure, and without the mediation of language or law. He describes the radicality of this otherness as 'otherwise than being', or an exteriority which is unrelatable to the self in any way. As such it is an experience 'overwhelming of intentionality' (Levinas, 1986a: 353).

Levinas prioritizes ethics ahead of philosophical thought and the primacy it gives to the self. In his writing the concept of existence is subordinate to the transcendence of an otherness which is not definable in terms of identity. Levinas makes his challenge to the philosophical privileging of self within the context of the centrality of metaphors of light and vision in the history of Western philosophy. As is the case with Merleau-Ponty, much of Levinas's work is an engagement with and response to the phenomenological systems of Husserl and Heidegger. Levinas engages critically with the ideal existence of consciousness in Husserl's phenomenology and with Being in Heidegger's phenomenology. However, I will not be discussing Levinas's work in direct relation to either of these two philosophers.[1] I will be focusing on the extent to which Levinas relies on touch as a sense that is distinct from vision in his articulation of an undertaking of sensibility which is prior to phenomenological discrimination.

In Merleau-Ponty's ontology, otherness is experienced temporally in the lived time of the self perceiving itself in its difference. In Levinas's account of ethical difference, the other is experienced as a non-synchronous separated other whose temporality interrupts the time of universal history with a time that cannot be recuperated. Derrida describes Levinas's philosophy as an attempt to locate radical heteronomy – as the desire for a thought of original difference (Derrida, 1978: 90). In his early writings Levinas uses the term 'alterity' to express absolute otherness. In *Totality and Infinity* (1979) he thinks this difference spatially in the term 'exteriority' (the book is subtitled 'An Essay on Exteriority'). In *Otherwise than Being or Beyond Essence* (1981) and in his most recent work he uses 'Other' (*l'autrui*, the personal Other, or you), reflecting his turn to language for the expression of radical difference.[2]

The absolute past of *an-archē* is referred to by Levinas as the 'trace' – a concept which although fundamental to Levinas's philosophy is certainly not unique. Derrida acknowledges his debt to Levinas, as well as his distance from him, in their differing conceptualization of the trace (Derrida, 1991b). Irene E. Harvey gives a comparative analysis of the trace as it circulates within the work of Husserl and Freud, as well as Derrida and Levinas (1986: 163–81). In Husserl, the trace is related to an originary temporalization which constitutes the 'Now', or condition of possibility of perception. In Freud it is related to the written trace, or structure of the mystic writing pad. In Derrida, the trace is theorized as *différance*. Levinas employs the trace to insist on an infinity which always exceeds the possibility of appropriation within consciousness. This infinity alters consciousness in evading the possibility of ever becoming the same.

Joseph Libertson identifies many parallels between Levinas's work and that of two of his contemporaries, Bataille and Blanchot. Like both these writers, Levinas's interest in subjectivity and its situation within being centres on differentiation rather than on illumination. Differentiation, unlike illumination, is not dependent on distance, but on dispossession. In every instance of consciousness which Levinas considers, be it the subjectivity of sensation in *Otherwise than Being or Beyond Essence* or the subjectivity of *jouissance* in *Totality and Infinity*, consciousness is subject to an exteriority which is refractory to manifestation (Libertson, 1982: 32). Rather than consciousness, the foundation of being in the world is theorized as an alterity which is irreducible to it.

Instead of ambiguity, Levinas argues that there is a fundamental dispossession or exteriority of origin underlining the totality of the visual. Levinas describes the visible as the supremely precarious investment in the commonality of sensibility. The body in its sensible being is secondary to a sociality determined by the transcendence of an other whose singularity is unaccountable in terms of a universal visibility. For Levinas, the visual is the sense *par excellence* in which consciousness polarizes itself from the exteriority with which it is implicated. Levinas distinguishes between the qualitative presence of the visual as a totality limited by its dependence on an indefinable materiality, and proximity as the infinity of unthematizable disjunction. It is by means of the latter that Levinas conceives of an originary, transcendent other, in ethical rather than ontological terms. Proximity, which is the term around which Levinas bases his ethics, is a subjection to alterity before subjectivity can be posited as the locus of its own manifestation.

Unlike Merleau-Ponty, for Levinas the advent of consciousness is an opening without recovery. This is not a being given to oneself, but a being given over without initiative. Consciousness is infinitely passive in its beginning. Levinas describes it as a subjection by unthematizable anonymous otherness against which it is not possible to distance or position oneself. The exteriority of this otherness affects consciousness rather than underlies or mediates the presentability of visual phenomena. Levinas describes the subjection of proximity as a heteronomy, not in terms of the vagaries of subject and object of visual phenomena, but as an unrecoverable departure from, or space in time. This departure is thematized in the caress as a giving up of the body in its sensible being in favour of an interlude of anonymity. Instead of illumination, in the erotic encounter there is an obsessive involvement with the discontinuity or the loss of any conscious hold over an otherness which itself has no formal basis or power.

Despite having been acknowledged as an important influence by a number of intellectuals ranging from Lyotard, Derrida, Klossowski, Blanchot and Deleuze, Levinas is not a philosopher who is widely known outside France. Also, apart from Simone de Beauvoir's summation of Levinas's account of sexual relations as a self-interested objectification of women (1972: 16n), Levinas's work has not figured widely in feminist scholarship. However, his concept of radical heteronomy has significantly influenced Luce Irigaray in her formulation of an ethics of sexual difference.[3] Although, like de Beauvoir, Irigaray is critical of Levinas's theorizing of the feminine, her interpretation of his ethics is more attentive to the contradictions which beset his attempt to subordinate sexual difference to his account of ethical difference. As will be discussed in the following chapters, Irigaray's reading of Levinas's conceptualization of alterity is turned to a reconsideration of sexual difference as the threshold of ethics. It is also possible to draw from this reading an investment in light as a medium of feminine incarnation.

77

7

Scintillating Lighting

The sensuousness of light

For Levinas, existence in the world is defined as the sphere of light. Light is the sensuous element within which consciousness finds and sustains itself, and makes itself at home. Light is 'first experience', or the condition of the apprehensibility of sensibility. Levinas's analysis of the subject of light is based in part on Husserl's account of the intentional structure of consciousness.[1] This intentionality is preserved in Merleau-Ponty's phenomenal account of light as 'lighting', or bodily intentionality as the assumed intermediary of the unfolding of self and its enfolding within the sensible world. For Merleau-Ponty the sensation of light, as with all sensibility, comes into being 'within the framework of a certain setting in relation to the world which is the definition of my body' (1962: 303).

In keeping with Merleau-Ponty's assertion of the fundamental narcissism of vision Levinas regards the phenomenologically given world as a self-defined totality. As Derrida describes this apparent totality: '[e]verything given to me within light appears as given to myself by myself' (1978: 92). The lucidity of things and ideas is primarily the egoism of finding oneself in the light. For Levinas, any emanation of light, from either the sensible or the intelligible (Platonic) sun, belies the desire to take hold of something or appropriate something for oneself which lies at the origin of phenomenological sense. As intentionality, sensibility has a possessive structure which is determined by the graspability of things. Light is the medium which sustains and bridges the difference between a subject of perception and perceivable things: 'Light makes objects into a world, that is, makes them belong to us' (Levinas, 1978a: 48).

Levinas theorizes light as the emergence of a separate existence through a polarization in which the self appears present to itself. The egoism of intentionality is based on the establishment of a sense of being at the centre of a panoramic objective world. The reflexivity of 'lighting' is a dual projection and enveloping of the world, or an appropriation of existence within the law of the Same. Likewise, intellectual apprehension is sense, understood in terms of the luminosity of light relative to the mind which desires clarity for itself:

> Light makes possible . . . this enveloping of the exterior by the inward, which is the very structure of the cogito and of sense. Thought is always clarity or the dawning of a light. The miracle of light is the essence of thought: due to the light an object, while coming from without, is already ours in the horizon which precedes it; it comes from an exterior already apprehended and comes into being as though it came from us, as though commanded by our freedom.
>
> (Levinas, 1978a: 48)

Light dawns as the chiasmic coincidence of exteriority and interiority in the moment of illumination. The exteriority of things is circumscribed by the being that embraces them. This ego distinguishes itself from its object as a light source always held in reserve. On the other hand, the exteriority of things is underlined by a givenness that, as with Platonic anamnesis (knowledge as recollection), awaits our apprehension.

Equally, the subject which comes into being in this totality is possessed by the light. Levinas distinguishes between the transcendental ego and the ego of sensuous enjoyment. Enjoyment is the ego at home with itself in the world, incorporated with the sensible in a way which deformalizes any notion of an intentionally defined separation of the subject in the world (Levinas, 1979: 115). The light which fills and maintains the interval of separation is also the medium of our substantial immersion in life. Sensuousness is a receptivity to existence at the level of its elemental materiality. Levinas finds this form of egoism in the structure of enjoyment, or an experience of self based on its dependence on the material world:

> Life is *love of life*, a relation with contents that are not my being but more dear than my being: thinking, eating, sleeping, reading, working, warming oneself in the sun. Distinct from my substance but constituting it, these contents make up the worth [*prix*] of my life.
>
> (Levinas, 1979: 112)

Our affective lives begin with our bodies' elemental participation in light, air and water as media whose worth is not determinable as information, recollectable data or unifiable multiplicities. As a sensuous element, light is a medium in which we are able to sustain and enjoy ourselves.

For Levinas, enjoyment is the pleasure derived from the satisfaction of needs. The paradigm of this form of egoism is alimentation. The activity of nourishing oneself by incorporating or assimilating the non-self into the same as one's self is the accomplishment of enjoyment: 'We live from "good soup," air, light, spectacles, work, ideas, sleep, etc.' (1979: 110). Humanity thrives on need. Its self-interestedness binds human beings into economic communities, within whose structures individuals relate to one another in order, ideally, to satisfy their mutual needs. 'Living on' is neither a state of freedom (because it is a dependent freedom) nor a dependence (because it is enlivened by its own necessity). It is a form of identity which is constituted as the same as, rather than dependent on or in opposition to, the non-self.

Levinas disagrees with the Platonic denunciation of the illusory nature of the satisfaction that can be generated by need (1979: 116). The lack which satisfaction makes good for Plato is a negative notion of need. Instead, Levinas describes a self-sufficient ego which withdraws into itself in the state of enjoyment. Enjoyment is an autoaffective structure, not a state mediated by an ideal self. It is an internalizing movement which Levinas describes as a 'coiling' into a self (1979: 118). Being at home with itself is an immediacy which comes from its assimilation of the other on the basis of need. The pleasures and pains of enjoyment and need are uniquely engendered in the solitary self. This is a state of existence whose autonomy does not lie in its assumption of being, but in the enjoyment of its capacity for enjoyment (a plenitude which does not exceed itself): '[f]or the I to be means neither to oppose nor to represent something to itself, nor to use something, nor to aspire to something, but to enjoy something' (1979: 120). The narcissism which springs from need is corporeality savouring the agreeableness (agreement to assimilation) of its own substantiality.

Based on this autoaffective mechanism, Levinas argues that sensuousness is of the order of enjoyment rather than the order of experience (1979: 137). Experience is 'experience of' something, and as such is representational. According to Levinas, representation consists in the possibility of accounting for something as though it was an idea, or reducible to a product of thought. Sensuousness is the co-existence of a body and a world. Levinas associates the subject of experience and thought with sound, or a hearkening to oneself, rather than to the chiasmic coincidence of exteriority and interiority in the sensuousness of light (1979: 128).

Unlike the experience of something, sensuousness is an unreflective undertaking, and is unrelated to thought. Sensuousness has no object in mind. Its aim and end is to gratify need, which is satisfiable without resort to the representation of a source: 'One does not know, one lives sensible qualities: the green of these leaves, the red of this sunset. Objects *content* me in their finitude, without appearing to me on a ground of infinity' (1979: 135). In embracing its dependency and thereby internalizing or becoming content, corporeality is a constant challenge to the assumption that the attribution of meaning is the preserve of consciousness. The formulation of meaning changes sense in the living body, for which sensibility is not an experience with an absent referent, but a condition: 'I but open my eyes and already enjoy the spectacle' (1979: 130).[2] In sensuousness, things only take form within the medium in which they are constituted: 'Every relation or possession is situated within the non-possessable which envelops or contains without being able to be contained or enveloped. We shall call it the elemental' (1979: 131). Like the surface of the sea or the edge of the wind, these sensations are indeterminate, elemental, formless, without beginning or end. Levinas finds this distinction implicit in Cartesian mind/body dualism, which acknowledges the uniqueness of sensibility in its refusal to give sense data the status of clear and distinct ideas (1979: 129–31). The unrepresentable source of enjoyment is of no concern to enjoyment. Need is its only grounds, and nourishment a 'happy chance' (1979: 141).

The subject of light is an egoistic totality which is only qualitatively present in the indeterminate sameness of self and other in sensuous existence. Levinas maintains that it is not possible to experience sensuous existence objectively, as a something else, emphasizing instead the dependent nature of this existence. Bodily intentionality is expressed by Levinas in terms of an appeasable appetite. In the enjoyment of itself as a living entity, sensibility is an egoism which bespeaks a participation in the elemental which is not yet (re)cognizable. Instead the self is a monadic being that takes up or assumes an existence only in its carnal constitution.

The restlessness of night

In his early work, Levinas considers the separateness of the ego of light in terms of *hypostasis* or as an entity; a subject of the verb *to be*; the event by which the act expressed by a verb becomes a being designated by a substantive. However,

Levinas wants to break with the ontological basis of this philosophical term, and the various shifts in his work trace his development of different strategies with which to address the problem. In the essays collected together in *Existence and Existents* (1978a) Levinas explores the Platonic notion of an ideal beyond existence as a movement which leads to an ideal beyond light. In Levinas's ethics, the challenge to hypostasis is not conceived of as a transcendence towards a superior being, but an *ex-cendence*, or departure from the light of being. Derrida's comment in response to Levinas's approach is that in attempting to philosophize without light Levinas is confronted at the outset with a certain dilemma: 'it is difficult to maintain a philosophical discourse against light' (Derrida, 1978: 85–6). To do away with the violence of a universality of light for the sake of ethics would be to abandon what to philosophy appears to be the natural means for counteracting the blindness of mysticism and the violence of history. It would also be to base ethics on the martyrdom of Reason (Harvey, 1986: 227).

Levinas approaches the dilemma by playing on the double qualities of the Platonic sun as that which both creates and destroys the relation between language and presence. This is a strategy which parallels Bataille's emphasis on the duplicity of solar forces.[3] As well as a source of illumination, Bataille emphasizes the destructive, burning, wastefulness of the sun. While Bataille develops a form of expression based on the concept of a rotten carnal sun devoid of light, Levinas turns from the sun in search of a nocturnal powerless source of light. Levinas begins his difficult task by reconsidering the limited freedom of the ego as a self-defined totality:

> The *I* always has one foot caught in its own existence. Outside in face of everything, it is inside of itself, tied to itself. It is forever bound to the existence which it has taken up. This impossibility for the ego to not be a self constitutes the underlying tragic element in the ego, the fact that it is riveted to its own being.
>
> (Levinas, 1978a: 84)

As well as discussing the egoism of enjoyment, Levinas draws upon the significance of its adherence to the elemental. The pleasure derived in enjoyment also reveals that the materiality which determines the ego is also something which it is not:

> what is distinctive about the sovereignty of the I that vibrates in enjoyment is that it is steeped in a medium and consequently undergoes *influences*. The

originality of influence lies in that [sic] the autonomous being of enjoyment can be discovered, in this very enjoyment to which it cleaves, to be determined by what it is not, but without enjoyment being broken up, without violence being produced. It appears as the product of the medium in which, however, it bathes, self-sufficient. Autochthony is at the same time an attribute of sovereignty and of submission; they are simultaneous. What has influence over life seeps into it like a sweet poison.

(Levinas, 1979: 164)

The dependence of the ego on the elemental is as much an affliction as it is a source of enjoyment. In its elemental existence the ego is a pure substantive. In the endurance of this substance in pain, sensibility is reduced to matter. Pain demonstrates that the ego is not based on any assumptions about the substantiality of its existence, but that it exists, inescapably, substantially. To give an example of what Levinas means by the ego's substantiality: light is not merely something to be enjoyed; the ego can perish from exposure to the elemental. A body can be burned and blinded and, in the case of lasers, cut by light.

In order to account for the ego's dependence on an 'exteriority' which is not reducible to intentionality but, as for example in the case of pain, reduces sensibility to a passive endurance, Levinas takes up the purely affective dimension of anonymous existence. He seeks the evidence of this exteriority in the anonymity of the elemental, or an undifferentiated substantive. Rather than an indeterminate other, which is reduced to the ends of enjoyment, anonymous existence is the singling out of the substantive as a pure verb, a pure enduring in the very anonymity of being backed up on itself. This is a presence without content, in a state of sensitivity rather than of sensuousness.[4]

Levinas distinguishes between the anonymity of perception and anonymous sensibility. This is a distinction which marks Levinas's departure from Merleau-Ponty's theorization of perception. Levinas maintains that perception cannot be based on an anonymous sensibility. For Levinas, perception is the sensibility of intentionality, which means that it is neither based on nor takes the form of an indeterminate sensibility. For Merleau-Ponty there is a lapsing of the self in this indeterminate sensibility. For Levinas there is no lapsing in the anonymity of indeterminate sensibility. Levinas distinguishes between the night of anonymous existence and a phenomenological night as the opposite of day(light). This latter night is a dimming of the light, which means the disappearance of things from sight, the lapse of consciousness in sleep, or the night of dreams.[5] Here the absence of light is a night of concealment, a loss of visibility, or an obscuring of illumination.

The night of anonymous existence, on the other hand, is unrelated to light and its phenomena. Unlike the manifestations of consciousness, the purely affective dimension of anonymous existence emerges in the total exclusion of light, and is devoid of things and distance. This is the indeterminacy of nocturnal space, which is not empty, but a presence 'full of the nothingness of everything' (Levinas, 1978a: 58). The void of night is an absolutely unavoidable *there is* (*il y a*). The term *there is* refers to an anonymous being in general which persists without anything or anyone being there.[6] Rather than the absence of light as concealment, *there is* exposes the subject of hypostasis to a difference which resists incorporation, or to a presence without a substantive: 'nothing approaches, nothing comes, nothing threatens; this silence, this tranquility, this void of sensations constitutes a mute, absolutely indeterminate menace. The indeterminateness constitutes its acuteness' (1978a: 59).

It is not possible to distance oneself, position oneself, withdraw into oneself in the face of this unapprehendable impersonal immediacy. Anonymous existence is being exposed, invaded, submerged, given (indistinguishably) in the night. The presence of night is both without interval and an interval which is refractory to the distinction required for illumination. The paradigmatic endurance of this condition of undifferentiated consciousness is the relentless monotony of insomnia, as an inability to close one's eyes and find oblivion, and yet an inability to see. The *there is* or 'it' which is neither avoidable nor illuminating is a 'nothing to see' which is indefinable in terms of the consciousness of phenomena. Rather than having 'a night to oneself' in the lapsing of consciousness into unconsciousness and sleep, the indeterminacy of insomnia is wakefulness without manifestation (1978a: 65–6).

For Levinas, the nothingness of *there is* is the key to the meaning of horror. Horror is the term he draws upon to counter Heidegger's proposition of the ego's anguish and anxiety in the face of nothingness.[7] Levinas does not equate horror with nothingness as a fear of death. Horror is the fear of an invading and persistent nothing which cannot be negated. Horror overwhelms consciousness with a closeness that is suffocating, pervading and contaminating but whose materiality has no correlation with oneself:

> horror turns the subjectivity of the subject, his particularity qua *entity*, inside out. It is a participation in the *there is*, in the *there is* which returns in the heart of every negation, in the *there is* that has 'no exits.' It is, if we may

say so, the impossibility of death, the universality of existence even in its annihilation.

(Levinas, 1978a: 61)

Consciousness and its phantasmagoria are not the source of the horror of this night, alive without end. The reverse is the case; consciousness sweats in the night itself that watches in the absence of light (1978a: 66). The presence of night – a collapse of things into indeterminate nothing, a horror which can also occur in the midst of daylight – erodes the continuity of consciousness. This passivity which encroaches without appearing is the means by which Levinas expresses his proposition of the *there is* as 'existence in general', or a non-visual, non-ontological precursor of presence. *There is* (also referred to in Levinas's work as alterity, illeity, the trace of the Other) cannot be reduced to the totality of egological understanding, but persists as a participation with an exterior which is extraneous to the finitude of 'lighting'.

The interval of night in Levinas's conception is not an indeterminacy or ambiguity of light. It is an anonymity which is uninterruptible, never revealed or concealed in lighting. The subject of light or the ego is defined as a positioning, whose lapses and returns are a respite or time from this infinite anonymity:

> the appearance of the existent is the very constitution of a mastery, of a freedom in an existing that by itself would remain fundamentally anonymous. In order for there to be an existent in this anonymous existing, it is necessary that a departure from the self and a return to the self – that is, that the very work of identity – become possible. Through its identification the existent is already closed up upon itself; it is a monad and a solitude.

(Levinas, 1987b: 52)

The present referred to in this passage is the constant undertaking of the event of hypostasis, which Levinas characterizes as the establishment of presence: 'The present rips apart and joins together again; it begins; it is beginning itself' (1987b: 52). Hypostasis is a tear, a moment of consciousness, a materialization of the otherwise unending anonymous *there is*. The escape from the horror of the *there is* is a recoiling into the finitude of solitary existence. The horror of this anonymity is averted in the violence of consciousness.

Rather than a presupposition, Levinas argues that consciousness is a condition, or position, based on a passive subjection. Light is a scintillating

85

phenomenon, harbouring an anonymous contaminating materiality in the oscillations of consciousness. Immobilized by the limitlessness of night, consciousness is the turning of this immobilization into a base, a stance, a self, a *here* or recess in the *there is*: 'Position is not added to consciousness like an act that it decides on; it is out of position, out of an immobility, that consciousness comes to itself' (1978a: 70). Each spark of light is a fixation of its surrender to the impersonal night; each conscious moment a night suspended in light's sparkling hesitations. The abandonment of a position is a dissipation of light, a disintegration of the subject into the *there is*. Night is the dis-*aster* of which Blanchot writes; an abandoning of the firmament of vision, and with it a dimming of an enlightened consciousness reflected in the starry heavens (Blanchot, 1986).

The importance of night in Levinas's theorization of vision is that it sus-*tains* the transparency of light. Light is a not an absolute certainty, but a tenuous condition. Rather than a source of clarity, light is the effect of immobilization:

The contact with light, the act of opening one's eyes, the lighting up of bare sensation, are apparently outside any relationship, and do not take form like answers to questions. Light illuminates and is naturally understood; it is comprehension itself. But within this natural correlation between us and the world, in a sort of doubling back, a question arises, a being surprised by this illumination. The wonder which Plato put at the origin of philosophy is an astonishment before the natural and the intelligible. It is the very intelligibility of light that is astonishing; light is doubled up with a night.

(Levinas, 1978a: 22)

Night differs from Merleau-Ponty's chiasm of light in so far as night's invisibility breaks open the indeterminacy of phenomenological light. Night reveals the limits of phenomenology in the body's carnality. The confrontation with anonymous carnality is a dissipation of self, which can only be avoided by encountering some thing other than this amorphousness. The wonder of light is the absolute coincidence of something other – an undefinable being – with self, an instance of intelligibility, momentarily suspending the anonymity of materiality in the apparition of presence. Light, whether it be the light of dreams, reason, or the mapping of the universe in light years, is an immobilization of *there is*. Away from the anonymity of night, light is the totality of the position we find ourselves in.

By referring to lighting as scintillation Levinas limits consciousness to the place which it establishes for itself rather than a locus in an abstract space.

Existence has a concrete setting in one's own body as a place. To leave this place is to lose oneself, to dissolve into the anonymous *there is*. It is not as materiality, but in the realization of itself in its materiality, that the sub-*stance* of the body is taken as an event – the event of position – here. The body, as the event of position, is the very advent of consciousness. Levinas rejects the dualist notion that consciousness can be divorced from a substantive. Consciousness begins as a sense of corporeality; as a sense of consciousness's base or place, its point of departure, the condition of its inwardness or in-stance.

Levinas uses night to describe a state of dispossession which underlies all sensibility, not only vision. To explain further the point which Levinas makes, comparison can be made between the absence of vision in the night, and blindness. The affective state of eyes which are unable either to close or see in the night is not the same as eyes that have been blinded. Blindness, as an 'unseeing in the eye', has been treated abstractly in philosophy as a quality of knowing, whether as innocence, denial, madness, sacred and apocalyptic insight or ignorance. Alternatively, it has been treated as a differential form of knowing, achieved by the supplanting of vision by other senses. From Locke's argument that a man born blind and restored to sight would not be able to recognize visually what was familiar to touch, to Diderot's argument that blindness favours relational rather than representational thought, blindness has been regarded as a difference in understanding rather than an absence of sight. As an otherwise potentially unknown difference of thought in a visually constituted symbolic order, blindness has also been granted an imaginary transparency by the possibility of cure, with a potentiality for conversion to the universality of sight (see Paulson, 1987).

Blindness, as an inability to see, is defined in relationship to the grasping of things. As such it, and all the senses recruited in its place, are dependent on even if they differ with the presuppositions of illumination. Levinas adds another dimension of unseeing to the eye. Instead of the cessation of vision, the unavoidable *there is* extends the lack of sight beyond the inability to see. The indeterminate nothing which dissolves sight into a useless state leaves the eye defenceless and exposed to the inexhaustibility of an other impersonal being. The best-known development of an unmitigated attentiveness to an otherness in the night which interrupts the consistency of egological existence is found in the literary works of Bataille and Blanchot, who both describe eyes which take on powers of extraordinary proportions when penetrated by an irreducible materiality which prevents them from seeing (see Libertson, 1982: 205–8).

The expressive body – the face

Levinas's proposition of an otherness that transcends egological existence is thematized in the face. In his adoption of the face as an otherwise than phenomenologically definable experience, Levinas is also negotiating and challenging many philosophical propositions based on analogies of the face. Levinas's argument rests on the imperative attendant in the uniqueness of the face, rather than making use of the face as an analogy. The use of analogies of the face is secondary to or trades on the singularity of this command. The face must be divorced from the Hegelian specularity of intersubjective recognition. Instead of a figure of rationalizable commensurability or mutual recognition, the face is an incommensurability which effaces, or suspends, the possibility of reciprocity through recognition. The expression of the face must also be distinguished from the broader humanist tradition of associating the face and the eyes with the mirrors of the soul, or body parts which have the power to express and to communicate what is inward. Such associations perpetuate the fantasy of transparent face-to face encounters (Levinas, 1978a: 72).[8] For Levinas the face is not a sign of something; it is the exposition of signification. Levinas considers that the face as a mode of regard is not founded on visual perception. Instead, to regard means not only to look but also to have regard, or give particular care. Looking is the condition of sight, a violation which incorporates an object into the field of one's gaze. Regard is a generosity towards the face in its material particularity. Over and above its presentation as an image, the face is an irreducible other, which eludes the speculation of the gaze:

> The way in which the other presents himself, exceeding *the idea of the other in me*, we here name face. This *mode* does not consist in figuring as a theme under my gaze, in spreading itself forth as a set of qualities forming an image. The face of the Other at each moment destroys and overflows the plastic image it leaves me, the idea existing to my own measure and to the measure of its *ideatum* – the adequate idea. It does not manifest itself by these qualities. . . . It *expresses itself*.
>
> (Levinas, 1979: 50–1)

The face is a crossing within the totality of vision to the inadequacy of the discursive. Levinas draws a distinction between the violence of vision as a habitual immobilization and incorporation of difference, and the transformation of the 'avidity of the gaze' into a generous ear for the other's voice. Levinas's project is to recount the scope of this 'eye that listens' in terms otherwise than the resonance of essence or the reverberation of light (1981: 30). In encountering the face, the eye ceases to see difference in terms of its possibilities for negation. It becomes a seeking for the means to do justice to the other's singularity.

As a persistence of difference which cannot be grasped, the face simultaneously prolongs and falls short of the sur-facing of sight. While apparently similar to Merleau-Ponty's argument that the self cannot grasp its own act of grasping, Levinas's argument is that the face is a trauma that cannot be represented. Rather than an eclipse of sight, the subject of light is indebted, without apprehension, to the anarchy of the face. The anarchy of the face is an infinite difference, theorized by Levinas as a never presentable deferred identity, or difference as a non-recurrence, as always already past. The effacement of the face is the trace of an indefinable other, which Derrida elaborates in his deconstruction of the idea of origin. However, in his thematization of alterity in the face, Levinas places an emphasis on the radical singularity of the trace.[9] The trace is a difference whose ungraspability does not derive from the economy of difference. Singularity, unlike individuality, is not defined within the logic of the universal, where one term is other in relation to all the rest. The uniqueness of the other's face is an excess which resists totalization. Richard A. Cohen lists the four component terms of this excess as follows: first, the alterity of the other person; second, the passivity of the self, and their 'relations'; third, the other's command; and, fourth, my responsibility to respond (Cohen, 1986: 6). Devoid of systematic character, uncontainable and incomprehensible, the other's face is a strangeness, a transcendence of the other which requires a response which is different from recognition or knowing.[10]

In Levinas's work the relationship between subject and other commences in the inequality of their terms. In this inequality, each term is transcendent to the other. Alterity is what constitutes the identity of each. The relationship is produced between unequal singularities and precludes the possibility of there being an exterior or third party or universal which could incorporate them (Levinas, 1979: 251). The subject can never identify with the other, only respond to and provide for the other's needs. To be a self is to be a subject in the accusative – not 'I think' or 'I see', but 'Here I am'. The other impels the acknowledgement of one's responsibility, in responding to the other's address (Cohen, 1986: 8). In this sense Levinas inverts Kantian ethics by insisting that responsibility to others does not conflict with and demand the suspension of particular desires, but precedes and makes possible their realization (Lingis, 1986: 224).

Derrida challenges the proposition that alterity or the non-thematizability of the singular can be thematized in the face. As the experiencing of a presence of any kind, the presence of the face is textually defined. The unthematizable expresses itself as a figure which is always already thematized: 'Is not experience always an encountering of an irreducible presence, the perception of a phenomenality?' (Derrida, 1978: 152). For Levinas, there is no encounter of presence in the face. The face commands presence; it is experience *par excellence*. In work subsequent to *Totality and Infinity* Levinas does not refer to 'experience', which is the thematization of equivalence, but to 'transcendence', where the subject must answer for what has not been included in thematization (1978b: 189). The face-to-face is an asymmetrical, immediate, irreversible relation, in which the face of the other transcends all thematization. The face is a trauma or disturbance of presence rather than a perception of phenomenality. It is, beyond the egoism of existence, a visitation unpresupposable within the visible world.

This disturbance is neither a revelation nor a dissimulation of presence, but a bleeding without recovery.[11] In his second major work, *Otherwise than Being or Beyond Essence* (1981), Levinas attempts to avoid the problem of phenomenality which adheres to the face as a visible presence. He does this by refiguring the trace in terms of an apprehension which is unrelated to appearance. In his account of 'Saying' (*le dire*), Levinas finds a lacuna in the natural passage of the 'I' of representation from the particular to the universal. The pronominal *se* of Saying remains an accusative self, refractory to the resonance of the Said (*le dit*) (Levinas, 1981: 37–8).[12] The epiphany of the face presents for Levinas the challenge of proposing a sense of unapproachability which is 'prior to history'. The trace is a lapse, a departure, an insertion of space in time (Levinas, 1987a: 105). In the anarchy of the face the present falls out of synchrony with itself into diachrony, faced with the transcendence of another time which is incommensurable with the present. This lapse of time is a profoundly passive senescence, or a removal of time which can never return to the present. Unlike the recurrence of incarnation of the subject in the world, the lines of ageing on a face bear out its subjection to the unrecoverable passage of a never present, immemorial past (Levinas, 1981: 51–2).

While Levinas criticizes Merleau-Ponty for proposing the emergence of meaning from the obscurity of flesh (Levinas, 1990a: 60–6), Derrida criticizes Levinas for proposing a sense of infinity which is beyond the metaphysics of presence (Derrida, 1978: 152). The difficulty confronting Levinas is expressed by Derrida as a problem of light:

Who will ever dominate it, who will ever pronounce its meaning without being pronounced by it? What language will ever escape it? How, for example will the metaphysics of the face as the *epiphany* of the other free itself of light? Light perhaps has no opposite; if it does, it is certainly not night.

(Derrida, 1978: 92)

Levinas poses the question of ethics as, simultaneously, the inauguration of responsibility and the impossibility of its representation. The very proposition of the infinity of the face as an originary opening of the question of ethics is, according to Derrida, itself a metaphysically based presupposition. Derrida's criticism serves to highlight the difficulty which confronts Levinas in his proposition of an ahistorical responsibility in the singular, with no identificatory or perceptual basis.

Levinas approaches the trace as a disturbance, devoid of meaning, which irreparably interrupts and changes, rather than underlies phenomenological sense. As such, the face does not have a visibility which originates within the visible universe. The abstractness of the face founds discursivity, not visibility. One hears and speaks to a face. There is a voice supplanting its image. Its particularity is a heteronomy which commands a direct form of sociality of me, independently of rational discourse, without recourse to the possibility of the reverse command from me:

The face, the countenance, is the fact that a reality is opposed to me, opposed not in its manifestations, but as it were in its way of being, ontologically opposed. It is what resists me by its opposition and not what is opposed to me by its resistance. This means that this opposition is not revealed by its coming up against my freedom; it is an opposition prior to my freedom, which puts my freedom into action. It is not that to which I oppose myself, but what is opposed to me. It is an opposition inscribed in its presence before me. It does not follow my intervention; it opposes itself to me in so far as it turns to me.

(Levinas, 1987a: 19)

Before meaningful speech, the face 'speaks', signifying only itself: 'A face has a meaning not by virtue of the relationships in which it is found, but out of itself; that is what *expression* is' (1987a: 20). Derrida refers to this auto-referentiality as an 'unthinkable unity of a speech able to assist itself and a glance which calls for assistance' (Derrida, 1978: 106); but, however haunted by complicity with

91

phonocentric plenitude, Levinas means there to be no intentionality or force in the signifying of the face. It expresses itself as an invitation to speak, as an undoing of phenomenality, as a rending of the very sensible in which it expresses itself – which Levinas contrasts with the disclosure of communicable speech.[13] The epiphany of the face is a transcendence which is alive in its openness, constantly divesting itself of its formal presence, denuding and disrupting its own manifestation (Levinas, 1987a: 96).

In contrast to the violence of the gaze, the face confounds any intentionality in the nakedness of its look. For Levinas, the eyes interrupt the formal unity of the face as a phenomenon. In their absolute nakedness, the eyes of the other exceed my own vision. I will never see directly what the other sees, I will never see with their eyes. In looking back at me with a singularity inconvertible to my own consciousness, the openness of the face is an expression of welcome while demanding a response that calls the totality and security of my own position into question. Delivering a frustrating twist to the Hegelian opposition of warring consciousnesses, the face of the other has a defenceless vulnerability which commands me to offer my regard. The commandment is delivered without the force of signification. It is a command from a different time, a different place, from a totality which transcends my own. In the face of an absolute independence which disrupts my own, the only alternative to regard would be the total annihilation of the other's existence. Such action, when it is undertaken, is bound to fail. To kill this intolerable other would be to renounce comprehension completely; murder is left only with the sensible remains. Even in taking the other's life, the difference of the other would remain inviolable: 'Infinity presents itself as a face in the ethical resistance that paralyses my powers and from the depths of defenceless eyes rises firm and absolute in its nudity and destitution' (Levinas, 1979: 199–200).

The nakedness of the face has a rationality all of its own, as an invitation to either comprehend or murder, and a command to do neither. The face is seen in the light of a voice, which lends nothing to its visibility beyond resistance to disclosure:

> The light proper to expression, which enters into relationship with me through speech, this absoluteness of a thing in itself, revealed by the impossibility of murder, belongs neither to the order of the disclosure of forms, nor to that of irrational contact. It is rational, but with a rationality prior to all constitution. Expression is just this way of breaking loose, of coming toward us, yet without deriving its meaning from us, without being

a work of our freedom. If a face is not *known*, that is not because it does not have meaning; it is not known because its relationship with us does not refer to its constitution.

(Levinas, 1987a: 22)

The light of the face establishes the space for a virtually theological encounter with an other whose transcendence is refractory to self-interest, dogma or speculation. Rather than a light establishing its existence or visibility, the face is lit by a light which establishes discursivity. This light is a communication whose fragility exceeds the face's visibility. The light of the face has a gentleness which, while disrupting figuration, assumes the unapproachable proportions of divine command.

The extent to which Levinas poses the face as a quintessentially ethical challenge can be demonstrated by a qualified comparison with Walter Benjamin's political framing of the face's presentation.[14] Although he is a political rather than ethical theorist, like Levinas, Benjamin's interests centre on a retheorization of experience. Benjamin insists on the radical historicity of experience, including the organization of sense perception itself. He seeks to render this experience as the experience of truth, thereby regaining the fullness of the concept of experience of earlier philosophers, lost in the narrow subject–object paradigm of Kantian experience. The truthfulness of the present is the fundamental question that his philosophy of historical time addresses.[15] Levinas revises the primordial significance of infinity in metaphysics, in the process of which he is concerned to recover in philosophy a concept of experience surpassing the experience of meaning.[16] To that extent Levinas and Benjamin have a similar task in mind. However, a fundamental difference emerges between Levinas and Benjamin regarding their emphasis on the historicity of the organization of sense perception or the structuring of experience in its historical formation.

In his theorizing of the 'condition' of vision, Levinas verges on a genetic formulation which is indifferent to aspects of experience in modernity which Benjamin struggles to come to terms with. By way of contrast, Benjamin's interests are less directed to the ethics of self–other relations than to theorizing the communal experience of subject–object relations. For Benjamin, ways of experiencing are historico-socially imposed relations between a recipient and things which underlie conscious perception. In an effort to bring the unconscious presuppositions of understandability into play, Benjamin embarks on a project of making that which appears familiar into something strange, while rendering the unfamiliar familiar by drawing upon resonances with the past. While Benjamin's interest is directed in particular to novelty as it is fetishistically mass-produced in the culture of modernity, the central inflection he places on modernity's mode of operation is its spiritualization of the value of economic exchange in the reification of experience. In other words, the emphasis is not on spiritual values becoming commodified, but on commodities acquiring a face. 'Authentic' experience is transformed into a private, incommunicable disjunction with a shocking immediacy, disarticulated from and resistant to the economy of reproduction. Through its aura – the unique maintenance of distance, however close it may appear in its material aspect – the experience of a thing becomes identical with its authenticity, with an appearance refractory to human manufacture. The promise of auratic distance is the fetishistic promise of a participatory relation with nature which never comes to pass.

The relationship between auratic experience and the politics of cultural phenomena in Benjamin's work is an ambivalent one. On the one hand aura is a false distance, and on the other hand this false distancing offers a space for a dialogical relation with cultural phenomena. The most famous example of the experience of proximity as it is produced in the institution of art is found in his analysis of the destruction of aura in film.[17] Benjamin theorizes this ambivalent movement of proximity and distance as a function of the artwork's acquisition of a face. An alternative definition he gives for aura is an investment in an object's ability to return the gaze.

For Benjamin, as for Levinas, the face thematizes an element of humanity which is other than self-same in origin. Like Levinas, Benjamin envisions the experience of an irreducible other as an encounter which oscillates between redemption and death. The face of the other withstands the gaze. Aura is the perception of an unapproachable distance, exemplified in facial encounters, which is transposed on to a relationship with a non-human other, and experienced as an object's ability to return the gaze. To experience the aura of a phenomenon means to invest it with the capacity to look back at oneself: 'the camera records our likeness without returning our gaze. But looking at someone carries the implicit expectation that our look will be returned by the object of our gaze' (Benjamin, 1968: 188). Rebecca Comay draws attention to the difficulties of understanding the sense of such an economy. If looking is a 'gift', she asks, what kind of gift would it be that would carry with it the expectation of a reciprocation or counter-gift (Comay, 1992: 142)? In other words, the question arises as to what extent the auratic moment is inscribed within the economy of an egological or narcissistic order of the Same.

In Levinas's work the face, in looking back, refracts the possibility of symmetry in the face-to-face: 'This curvature of the intersubjective space inflects distance into elevation; it does not falsify being, but makes its truth first possible' (Levinas, 1979: 291). Benjamin's own answer to such a question is provided by his theorizing of the disruption of the specular economy in terms of the mimetic faculty. For Benjamin the expectation of a counter-gaze is associated with the mimetic faculty of finding opaque resemblances, rather than identical images, in an external nature that 'can open its eyes'.[18] Instead of appropriation, such similarities appear in a 'flash', which allows no opportunity for identification. They are a space in time. Resemblance invades the immediacy of the sensuous present with the anarchy of a textual moment: 'language may be seen as the highest level of mimetic behaviour and the most complete archive of nonsensuous similarity' (Benjamin, 1978: 335–6). The non-sensuousness of resemblance, which is the store of involuntary memory, is lost to conscious recollection, which can find nothing to incorporate. The sensuousness of light is interrupted and over-powered by the unanticipatable resemblance.

Such flashes are not sources of illumination. Their ungraspability reveals only a counter-gaze which transcends the anticipatory projection of the gaze. Drawing a parallel between Benjamin and Levinas, Comay argues that, far from reinforcing the egological order of the visible through the reciprocal exchange of looks, the auratic image has a fragile reality which opens up the space of reciprocity. The irreducibility of this reciprocity simultaneously opens the space for and undermines the possibility of symmetry. The essence of reciprocity is not symmetry, but the non-reciprocal interruption of the gaze, exemplified for Benjamin in the shyness of the early subjects of photography, who 'drew back' in the moment of being photographed.[19] The re-experience of aura in its transference to objects is a form of reminiscence whose originality exceeds reproduction, speculation and conscious control. Auratic experience does not operate at the level of adequation. It is breathed, not grasped. In short, auratic vision is theorized as the delay of memory; a delay which is never experienced but always already past.

Miriam Hansen (1987) comments on the peculiar temporality of Benjamin's auratic memory; whose unique manifestation in a non-human image is related, she argues, to Freud's notion of the 'uncanny'. Hansen argues that the auratic image is a daemonic double whose familiarity has a life-threatening strangeness rather than the anticipated identity of a narcissistic ego-ideal. Like the return of the repressed, it is remembered without ever having been seen before. Hansen argues that Benjamin's writing seems driven by a desire to reverse and rehearse a displacement of a utopian past. The difficulty of his task is to avoid succumbing to fetishistic illusions, while preserving the promise of a better nature or different self which such illusions sustain. The prerequisite of auratic experience is in fact a purposeful forgetting, which Hansen identifies as the activity upon which Benjamin pins his conceptualization of a dimension of reciprocity as a desire which transcends the fetishistic organization of the gaze. The conjuring of resemblances by the 'optical unconscious' refers to the distortion of a familiar gaze in the non-human, nameless appearance of things.[20] By means of this term, Benjamin proposes a mode of psychical ambivalence for tracing the auratic gaze as an absorption in the realization of missed fulfilment. Such an attitude breaks up the simplicity of the opposition of narcissistic proximity and fetishistic distance in the complacency of the gaze.

On the one hand, the political significance of the optical unconscious is that it introduces an awareness of temporality and historicity into the proximity and distance of the gaze. The clammy, claustrophobic experience of anonymous materiality, which for Levinas is the nameless *there is*, is theorized by Benjamin as the physiognomy of modern experience – an occluding of the gaze through the homogenizing erasure of origin in the given. On the other hand, Benjamin speculates that, despite its withering away in the cult of the commodity, auratic contact is renewed in all its revolutionary power, in the erotic eye contact which he characterizes as the distanced closeness of the eyes of the beloved. The attentiveness to a nameless reciprocity has a naked materiality in a lover's gaze. In this lacuna in the falsity of a restrictive economic organization of the gaze, it is possible to invest the gaze of the other with a better, timeless nature.

Benjamin calls the task of emancipatory art the transformation of aura into the trace, by which he means the elevation of aura to a non-nostalgic movement of a desire which does not desire satisfaction or the recovery of presence. Art would strive for the transformation of forces which evoke the private experience of aura into the object of a collective experience: 'The trace is the manifestation of a closeness however distanced it may be. The aura is the manifestation of a distance however close it may be. In trace we enter into the possession of the thing, in the aura the thing overpowers us' (Benjamin, 1982: 560).[21] For Levinas aura refers to the sensible divesting itself of its sensibility in becoming an idea, while the trace is the sensible as never apperceptible, or graspable as an idea (Levinas, 1981: 61). Benjamin suggests that aura can be transformed into the trace, where we enter into the open possession of things with the asymmetrical unthematizable possessiveness of lovers. Levinas argues that the trace is an opening before all voluntary or involuntary seizure. We are held by but cannot enter into the senescence of the trace. There is no possibility of universalization or historical appropriation of its alterity. It is always already before history. While it is full of the danger of an incontestable transcendental claim, Levinas aims to avoid the ontological pre-suppositions of unconscious or purposeful forgetfulness in his theorization of the singular, unrecoverable transcendence of the face.

8

The Lightness of Touch

Proximity – the maternal touch

Merleau-Ponty discusses touch in terms of the opening of a perceptual domain in which our sense of embodiment emerges. Levinas considers touch as the exposition of an affective involvement with others. For Levinas subjectivity is a subjection to alterity before it can be posited as the locus of its own manifestation. Proximity is the communication of an anarchic sensibility that occurs before the subject can gather itself into a position in relation to this otherness which cannot be assembled in a representational present. As has been discussed in the previous chapter, Levinas describes an anarchical sensibility in terms of vulnerability and enjoyment, or exposedness to a non-phenomenal other rather than in ideational terms. Prior to any consciousness of sensation and irreducible to it, proximity is a sensibility which is distinguished from the conjunction which occurs in experience and knowledge. Rather than being apprehended by the subject, proximity is a signifying of an expositional *there is* that is alien to but suspended in presence.

Joseph Libertson outlines some basic themes of proximity which operate in the work of not only Levinas, but also a range of post-Hegelian thinkers of non-negatable difference, from Blanchot and Bataille to Nietzsche, Freud, Proust and Artaud. First, proximity is a contaminating communication rather than a communication based on a relationship between subject and object. Second, subjectivity is infinitely passive in its exposition. Third, rather than describing a sense of adequation, there is an obsessive urgency and repetition of a rapport with alterity. Fourth, a heteronomous, compelling excess persists in negation. Fifth, the communion of proximity is an involvement which is irreducible to manifestation. Finally, proximity is an approach of an exteriority which itself has no power, but against which consciousness has no power (Libertson, 1982: 208).

For Levinas subjectivity is given over to sensibility as a pure passivity. This passivity is not an impassive state of inertia or oblivion. It is infinitely more passive than any act of holding back or failure of initiative. Subjectivity is lodged in a being preoccupied by others which has nothing in common with the substantial body of rational selfhood:

> Sensibility — the proximity, immediacy and restlessness which signify in it — is not constituted out of some apperception putting consciousness into relationship with a body. Incarnation is not a transcendental operation of a subject that is situated in the midst of the world it represents to itself; the sensible experience of the body is already and from the start incarnate. The sensible — maternity, vulnerability, apprehension — binds the node of incarnation into a plot larger than the apperception of self. In this plot I am bound to others before being tied to my body.
>
> (Levinas, 1981: 76)

Levinas characterizes the exposedness of sensibility in its passivity as a being held hostage, or being offered without self-defined cause, without having initiated or conditioned the offering: 'Proximity is the subject that approaches and consequently constitutes a relationship in which I participate as a term, but where I am more, or less, than a term' (1981: 82). In Levinas's account of proximity, the given is free of conscious determination. The freedom of consciousness is not defined in terms of autonomy. It is a freedom which is inescapable, one which must be borne without choice or control. Consciousness is an illusory freedom compared to the insistence of the exteriority of its possibility. The immediacy of sensation is underscored, as Levinas argues, by the fundamental alterity of the given. The non-initiative of sensibility is a signalling of passivity which is older than the active generosity of offering oneself. It is 'the flesh made word' in its being affected, or the body as an 'in itself through the Other' (1981: 94).

The adherence of touch and incarnation in Levinas's work is prefigured by Kant in his analysis of the signification of the senses. Kant divides the senses relatively into objective senses (touch, vision and hearing) which contribute to knowledge of objects in their externality, and subjective senses (taste and smell), through which objects are enjoyed according to one's own disposition: 'By touch, hearing and sight we *perceive* objects (on the surface); by taste and smell we *partake* of them (take them into ourselves)' (Kant, 1974: 33–7). The value of the senses for Kant is their delineation of a folded corporeal schema which establishes the interiority of perceptions and the exteriority of objects. In this context, vision is the noblest of the senses because it maintains the most emphatic exteriority of its object – it is most distanced from touch. The object of vision is mediated by light.

Kant values vision as a transcendental faculty that renders the difference between an object and its appearance equivalent. Vision, like reason, produces an ideal relation with an object which, through the mediation of light, can be perceived in its material absence. Any symmetry that occurs is only within reflective judgement. Hearing is likewise mediated, but by air. The exteriority of its object is preserved even as sound enters the ears' labyrinths, because the sound in itself conveys nothing but the meaning given it. Both these senses avoid the vagaries of the more subjective senses – taste and smell – where for example one's own saliva and breath are involved in mediation. Touch, however, is the sense which most troubled Kant. In its immediacy of perception, touch is the most important of the senses, but its certainty is also the grossest of pressures. There is no denying the contact involved, but no means of objectifying the experience. Touch is the sense most affected by its object (Derrida, 1981b: 19). Despite attenuating the extent of touch into the tips of the fingers – it is a credit to Kant's honour, according to Nietzsche, 'that he should expatiate on the peculiar properties of the sense of touch with the naïveté of a country parson!' (Nietzsche, 1969: 104) – Kant is unable to ignore that bodies are affected by while differentiated in their contiguous relations.

Although Kant does not refer to it explicitly, there is an equivocation in touch which he resolves by a distinction which is relaxed for the other senses. In general, sensibility has two moments: sensation, which can be referred to objects; and feeling, which has no cognitive associations, and refers only to one's own body. While vision and hearing, and taste and smell are only relatively divided in this respect, touch is radically split. As an objective sense, it is sensation in the fingertips. As a feeling it is a sixth or supplementary sense of vital sensations.[1] This is purely the feeling of the responsive parameters of one's flesh, from hot and cold to the thrill of gooseflesh (Kant, 1974: 33). For Kant the necessity of touch remains completely obscure. It is the basis of the objective senses, but in the directness of its relation to its object it has no means to be unaffected or impartial.[2]

Levinas also distinguishes between two forms of touch. Contact as sensation is a discriminating touch that is related to vision. Touch as a difference in contact cannot be phenomenologically embraced. The parameters of proximity are inestablishable in a way that is not aligned with the vagaries and intertwin-ings of the subjectivity and objectivity of phenomenal sense. Sight tends to polarize the exteriority with which it is implicated, arresting the materiality of the sensible in its totalizing embrace (Levinas, 1981: 63). The sensible, how-ever, persists in its passivity as an exteriority which approaches and is touched on. This exteriority is never broached or exhausted. Levinas refers to proximity as the exposition of an irreconcilable heteronomy, or an infinity – an otherness which cannot be embraced.

Proximity is a sensibility that is not resolved into a consciousness which is conscious of itself as an other, as is the case in Merleau-Ponty's doubling and refolding of the touching and the touched. In proximity touch is an infinitely intimate lightness. While there is nothing which can come closer, there is nothing to take hold of in its affective immediacy:

> To be in contact is neither to invest the other and annul his alterity, nor to suppress myself in the other. In contact itself the touching and the touched separate, as though the touch moved off, was always already other, did not have anything in common with me.
>
> (Levinas, 1981: 86)

Levinas is not concerned with touch in any phenomenal sense, as an ambiguity in sensation. Proximity is an obsession with the designation of sensation. It is both contact and an involvement with discontinuity for its own sake.

Levinas refers to maternity, by which he means an incessant bearing of alterity without recovery, as the paradigm of the sensibility of proximity. Maternity is bearing par excellence, or a carrying of responsibility, vulnerability and suffering that is pre-natal in so far as it is prior to being (Llewelyn, 1995: 146). For Levinas, maternity is a pre-ontological past, an Other that cannot be subordinated to the vicissitudes of representation and knowledge, images, or an exchange of information (1981: 79). It is, instead, a being affected, a being held without grasping, an incessant bearing without recovery. The maternal hostage bears the burden of supplying the needs of another, responding unconditionally to an outside alien demand for one's own body to be offered over as a source of the other's nourishment. Maternity for Levinas is a reversal of the autonomy of subjectivity, which enjoys its materiality by incorporation. While virility is the paradigm of consumption and inhabitation, maternity, 'for an other', is the paradigm of donation and signification.

The vulnerability or exposedness to the other at the level of the other's materiality, which is for Levinas the basis of subjectivity, is demonstrated in everyday life in the for-the-other of one's own materiality:

> Signification signifies . . . in nourishing, clothing, lodging, in maternal relations, in which matter shows itself for the first time in its material-ity . . . .
>
> It is because subjectivity is sensibility – an exposure to others, a vulnerability and a responsibility in the proximity of the others, the one-for-the-other, that is, signification . . . that a subject is of flesh and blood, a man that is hungry and eats, entrails in a skin, and thus capable of giving the bread out of his mouth, or giving his skin.
>
> (Levinas, 1981: 77)

This signification of subjectivity as sensibility is analysed by Levinas in the phenomenon of suffering. Levinas's ethics reverses Kantian ethics by proceed-ing from the singularity of responsibility to the other's materiality. For Levinas, one's life and one's awareness of being here are dependent on being singled out to answer and provide for a need which is not one's own, but upon which one's own life and existence depend. Suffering for Levinas is the supreme ethical principle of bearing another's burden of materiality as my own responsibility. The constitutional or congenital uselessness of suffering 'can take on a meaning, the only meaning to which suffering is susceptible, in becoming a suffering for the suffering – be it inexorable – of someone else' (1988: 159).

Levinas's theorization of maternity is related to an understanding of the feminine which he derives from Talmudic commentary on the essential con-tribution of women to the continuity of messianic history. In this history, morality has its own ontological weight, in which the emphasis of the founda-tion of ontology shifts from incorporation to donation. The feminine is the vocation of the 'one who does not conquer' or a selfless humanity, which rather than having a visibility or a presence in the universal is 'the light of [man's] eyes' (Levinas, 1969: 32–3). For Levinas the feminine is an aspect of human existence rather than a human existent or transcendent other. The feminine is existence as habitation – being at home with oneself – the familiar (1979: 155). This is an intimacy with (not an incorporation or an inhabitation of) the other.

Merleau-Ponty makes metaphoric use of maternity in his ontology of flesh. In his adoption of maternity as the paradigm of proximity, Levinas considers the feminine in terms of its pre-ontological function. In Levinas's work maternity does not refer to any woman, but to an ethical subjectivity. The feminine is the original manifestation of all kindness on earth rather than an ontological presence in its own right. As the concretization of human habitation, the feminine is the welcoming of the stranger-other. The donation of hospitality depicts the dimensions of interiority as one's own dwelling, which commences only in being open to a stranger's prior claim. The welcome of hospitality is an understanding communicated without words. The possibility of intersubjective relations is dependent on the establishment of this dimension of human intimacy. The feminine reveals itself in this familiarity, not the face. It is a welcoming of the stranger without regard, but in the interests of preserving the dimension of discretion, or a possibility of withdrawal. This space of self-withdrawal is a locus that is presupposed in the egoistic assumption of and separation from an objective world (Levinas, 1979: 154–5).

Levinas calls the maternal the commonest everyday demonstration of the ethical relation, but it is precisely at such a level that maternity becomes an issue which demonstrates a responsibility that impinges upon the humanity of women. Maternal subjectivity as opposed to ethical responsibility is based on the tenuous elision of a distinction between dependency and autonomy, in which being held hostage is the paradigm of responsible motherhood. Any deviation from the paradigm slides into an adversarial relationship in which the humanity of the infant is pitted against feminine autonomy. This construction of the maternal relation is perhaps most apparent in legal issues, which consider the relation in terms of the designation of autonomy and responsibility. For example, in instances where women have been found culpable of damaging their unborn children, the foetuses have been effectively construed as innocent victims, held as hostages rather than accommodated in their (hostage) mothers' wombs.[3]

Catherine Chalier interprets the function of the feminine in relation to Levinas's work as a calling into question the virility of being. The feminine is a disruption of being by selflessness: 'an identity without security and without guarantee' (Chalier, 1991: 128). The disruption of being by self-sacrifice is the meaning of the feminine in the human being. By way of contrast, Derrida argues that sacrifice is possible only within a schema of human virtue based on carnivorous virility (Derrida, 1991a). Also, this interpretation does not address the question which other commentators, including Luce Irigaray (1991b), Jacques Derrida (1991b) and Tina Chanter (1991) address to Levinas: whether the feminine is absolutely other and thus primary (transcendent), or secondary to ethics. The suspicion remains that, in calling into question the 'supreme lucidity and hence a supreme virility' of being,[4] Levinas preserves an opening for an ethically based transcendence which occurs at the expense of radical difference – that is, the subordination of feminine transcendence. This aspect of Levinas's ethics is most apparent in the final section of *Totality and Infinity*, titled 'Beyond the Face'. There, Levinas deals with the possibility of concretizing the relationship of transcendence, or non-indifference, in another self. In his account of self-transcendence Levinas distinguishes between the maternal-feminine other of human being and woman as the inviolate disingenuous, mysterious, seductive, dangerous eternal feminine of erotic love. While the maternal is the condition of human existence, the feminine as the embodiment of alterity is exemplified in the caress.

The caress

Levinas analyses the phenomenon of the feminine as a carnality which both transcends and is inadequate to signification.[5] His depiction of an obsessive communion with the feminine in the caress completes his phenomenology of night (Wyschogrod, 1974: 118–19). Levinas refers to this as a 'night' in which a sense of impersonal being is experienced as the anonymous restlessness of *there is*. The feminine belongs to the same order of existence. Levinas conceives of the feminine as an exorbitance that is less than nothing, or an enduring mystery outside of human history. For Levinas, this mystery which lies beyond the face is experienced in the erotic encounter. As the body loses its status as an existent in the night, it is exposed as an unsignifiable materiality in erotic nudity.

In proximity, Levinas outlines sensibility in terms of signification rather than incorporation. In carnal love the other appears as an object of need while also resisting incorporation and remaining entirely other. Love is an encounter of both lust and transcendence – an equivocation which Levinas focuses upon as the originality of the erotic (1981: 100–1). In Levinas's account of love, there is no question of possessing the other – possession would extinguish eros: 'The very value of love is the impossibility of reducing the other to myself, of coinciding into sameness. From an ethical perspective, two have a better time than one' (1986b: 22). Rather than simply an appeasable appetite the caress is a hunger which suffers from an inability to tell it: 'In a caress, what is there is sought as though it were not there, as though the skin were the trace of its own withdrawal, a languor still seeking, like an absence which, however, could not be more there' (1981: 90). Erotic intimacy is not an attempt to assimilate an irreducible other, but an obsessive delight in soliciting the alien, and losing it and one's own perspective simultaneously.

Levinas describes carnal intimacy as the most intense experience of alterity while at the same time confining it to an equivocation that, unlike the face, never gives way to either the ethical transcendent other or to the one-for-the-other of signification. Gayatri Chakravorty Spivak observes Levinas's adoption of an anachronistic 'equivocation' which has long applied to the civil duplicity that has been woman's only access to public life and visibility (Spivak, 1992). Although manifestly a form of sensibility within the domain of touch, the caress is theorized as the negative of light. Voluptuosity is an abandonment of sociability, a movement from corporeality into the invisible in favour of an amorphous and indefinable community. Erotic love takes place in the dark — away from rational sociality, turning clarity into ardour and night:

> what the caress seeks is not situated in a perspective and in the light of the graspable. The carnal, the tender par excellence correlative of the caress, the beloved, is to be identified neither with the body-thing of the physiologist, nor with the lived body [corps propre] of the 'I can,' nor with the body-expression, attendance at its own manifestation, or face. In the caress, a relation yet, in one aspect, sensible, the body already denudes itself of its very form, offering itself as erotic nudity. In the carnal given to tenderness, the body quits the status of an existent.
>
> (Levinas, 1979: 258)

In the anonymity of eroticism, the existent is relieved of the solitude of existing. The intensity of alterity is a delight in the frivolous, in the evasion of form and fixity of meaning. Carnal intimacy is the diffusion of formal identity which is sought out in the elusiveness of an encounter which cannot be located, fixed and given form. Paul Davies maps the caress as an alteration of sensibility rather than a break with sensibility in his analysis of the movement away from vision (Davies, 1993). He interprets Levinas's later work as a reading of the moments where consciousness can no longer be an object of phenomenological analysis but, instead, those moments where consciousness can only be described as implicated, obsessed and obligated.

When Levinas considers the evasiveness of the feminine in the caress, he does so in visual terms, accompanied by the attenuation of touch in his account of eroticism. In Levinas's characterization, the carnal, the feminine, withdraws from the harshness of the light. The caress is an obsession with a non-negatable difference which persists in the absence of light:

The caress is a mode of the subject's being, where the subject who is in contact with another goes beyond this contact. Contact as sensation is part of the world of light. But what is caressed is not touched, properly speaking. It is not the softness or warmth of the hand given in contact that the caress seeks. The seeking of the caress constitutes its essence by the fact that the caress does not know what it seeks. This 'not knowing', this fundamental disorder, is the essential . . . always other, always inaccessible, and always still to come. The caress is the anticipation of this pure future [avenir], without content. It is made up of this increase of hunger, of ever richer promises, opening new perspectives onto the ungraspable. It feeds on countless hungers.

(Levinas, 1987b: 89)

Levinas characterizes the resistance of the feminine to incorporation as a self-effacement which eludes the grasp. In going beyond contact, the caress is a losing sight of touch as sensation rather than a perpetuation of the tactile. As an erotic gesture the action of the hand in the caress can be located within the paradigm of the hand's blind venturing in its attempt to alter and bring the elemental to light,[6] that is, it is conceived by Levinas as the obverse of *groping*. This is not an encounter whose indefinability is an opening to a transcendent other (1979: 254). The caress is a disorder of light. Beyond and inadequate to language, the erotic encounter is an obsession with an eternally never-present other. To the extent that Levinas considers eroticism within a phenomenological paradigm, the caress is an allegory of night, a breaking up of sensibility rather than a bringing the ethical and the feminine together on the plane of eros.

Levinas's account of eroticism is grounded in the presupposition of a subject whose incarnation is bound to a desire for the abyss. Countering the characterization of desire in terms of lack, Levinas conceives of desire as a yearning for a breach of satisfaction and rupture of solipsistic existence through another whose alterity cannot be overcome. Eroticism is a loss of perspective. It does not aspire to the infinite transcendence required for desire, which is reserved for the absolute alterity of the divine. As an evasion of significance, the feminine can never take on the aspect of the divine for Levinas. The dimension of *intimacy* in the midst of existence is opened by the feminine, not the dimension of transcendence (1969: 37). The anarchy of eroticism is a simultaneous needful/desirable disruption of any ontological project. Eroticism relieves egoism of its stiflingly lonely project, the repetitive affirmation of a closed ipseity, of a being grafted to its incarnation in the world of light – but carnal intimacy is not an opening of the infinity of desire.

For Levinas, eroticism is the ex-static dissolution of corporeality, rather than the achievement of the fecundity of incarnation. Fecundity is a relation-ship in which self goes beyond itself in the time of an other. The child, in being both same and other, establishes a relationship with an absolute future, or a renewal of time in a future that is 'not yet' rather than mine. Levinas's association of love with the anarchy of eroticism is distinguished from romantic love, which he describes as love becoming its own end (1969: 36). Eroticism is also distinguished from the eros of philosophical passion. Philosophy as eros is an idea of the infinite. Unlike the impossibility of a caress beyond the caress, '[a] thought that thinks more than it thinks is a desire' (1987a: 56). Levinas subordinates the anarchy of eroticism to the propagation of desire: 'In fecundity the I transcends the world of light – not to dissolve into the anonymity of the *there is*, but in order to go further than the light, to go *elsewhere*' (1979: 268). Voluptuousness is time out, or an interruption in the time of being, and its inexpressibility is a communion contrary to any social relation. Fecundity, as a capacity for possessing a fate that is other than one's own, is an escape from the universal or time of history that is not achieved with, but away from the feminine. Self-transcendence is ultimately achieved in paternity while the maternal-feminine is irretrievably anarchic. The renewal of being lies in the discontinuity or transportation of egoism outside of itself, in the diachronous encounter with another self. The fecundity of existence is revealed in the proximity of the encounter of one's own face, no longer merely one's own, but also the face of a son (1979: 277).

This brief account of fecundity does not reflect the progressively more complex relationship between eroticism and responsibility which develops chronologically in Levinas's work.[7] There is a shift from a preoccupation with the erotic in his early writing, to a concern with the ethical in his conceptualization of fecundity in *Totality and Infinity*. Tina Chanter also notes that, while *Otherwise than Being or Beyond Essence* concentrates on maternity at the expense of feminine eroticism, in his most recent work there is a restate-ment of two earlier themes. These are that the transcendence of alterity starts with femininity, while the structure of transcendence starts with paternity. This reaffirmation of the feminine as originary difference indicates a renewed adherence to the alterity of the feminine rather than its subordination to the non-indifference of the ethical relation (Chanter, 1991: 133). As well as the temptation to suggest a correlation between stages in Levinas's own life and these shifts between ethical and sexual alterity, there is a temptation to explain the tensions in Levinas's conceptualization of feminine alterity in terms of these discrepancies. Alternatively, the shifts can be read as symptomatic of a tension within Levinas's account of feminine alterity. Commentators who engage with Levinas on this issue will be addressed in the following chapter.

In his earlier work Levinas states that the ethical and the feminine are brought together on the plane of eros, and cannot possibly be grasped in terms of light. In *Totality and Infinity* he describes the erotic relation in phenomen-ological terms. The phenomenological is a form of description which, as Levinas states in his earlier work, 'by definition cannot leave the sphere of light' (1978a: 85). Conceived of in phenomenological terms the ungraspability of the feminine is a foregone conclusion: 'It is not possible to grasp the alterity of the other, which is to shatter the definitiveness of the ego, in terms of any of the relationship[s] which characterize light' (1978a: 85). The caress is an encounter that is qualified by a (dis)engagement of vision. In going beyond the face, the caress oscillates between the feminine as the embodiment of alterity and the feminine as an interlude in light – an equivocation of the feminine in the caress that is less a limit to ethics than the insistence of absence in a dynamic of exceeding yet withdrawal from sensuous contact: 'what is caressed is not touched'(Levinas, 1987b: 89). Levinas's phenomenology of Eros perpetuates a vision of absence as it loses its grasp of the feminine. Instead of an ethical threshold, in the caress Levinas reduces the feminine to humanity's own carnal being, or to an alter ego that is left suspended in the anonymity of night.

9

Illuminating Passion

Fecundity and ethics

Several of Levinas's commentators raise questions concerning the qualification he makes between ethical and sexual difference in his work. Among these commentators, Irigaray is arguably the most attuned to the way that Levinas perpetuates a masculine ethical subjectivity in his gendering of the caress, at the expense of a fecundity that would be the threshold of the ethical. The evidence that Levinas's understanding of sexual difference is confined to an other who is defined in terms of himself is most apparent in his account of carnal intimacy. It is apparent from this account that Levinas's concerns lie with man's self-transcendence, which is a desire transcending the solipsistic world of light. This desire is realized between men, their sons and their gods, while the woman lover lives an anonymous existence as man's material other, eschewing the world of light.

The first of the dozen or so questions which Irigaray addresses to Levinas in an essay titled 'Questions to Emmanuel Levinas: On the Divinity of Love' is: 'Is there otherness outside of sexual difference?' (Irigaray, 1991b: 109). The question is intended to highlight both the need to address sexual difference as an ethical limit, and the extent to which Levinas's understanding of sexual difference in no way suggests an other who is not defined in terms of himself.[1] Instead of an otherness of impossible determination, 'the feminine appears as the underside or reverse side of man's aspiration toward the light, as its negative' (1991b: 109). Irigaray continues by taking up Levinas's comment that the caress is a 'fundamental disorder' which does not touch the other. Order, she observes, is restored with the transformation of the flesh into a temporality which includes himself, in his encounter with a son.

Irigaray notes that Levinas confines eroticism to a perverse phenomenological interlude. The alteration of sensibility of the caress is related in terms of the distantiation of a feminine other rather than a differentiation of lovers where each is transcendent to the other. Self-transcendence, on the other hand, is a category of existence which opens on to a metaphysical desire. The feminine is not an ethical other but the passive un-doing of a virile aspiration in relation to light. Levinas characterizes the resistance of the feminine to incorporation as a self-effacement which eludes the grasp. Irigaray maintains that in his subordination of sexual difference to ethical subjectivity Levinas preserves the opening for a patrilineally based ethical transcendence at the sacrifice of a feminine transcendence. Irigaray's consistent complaint is that Levinas considers sexual difference as secondary to ethics, naming maternity as the paradigm of ethical responsibility and paternity as the paradigm of self-transcendence.

Irigaray argues that the disorder of Levinas's ethics is that he loses any idea of the function of the other sex as an alterity irreducible to the self. She notes that there are at least two reasons for this. First, despite speaking of a loss of all distinctions, there is always a distance maintained with the other in his account of love. Rather than something 'im-mediate' produced together, between each other, by the lovers in their difference, as their shared pleasure or work or child, it is a one-sided distance of the self from its invisible other. Second, instead of the feminine other, Levinas uses the son to mediate the fecundity of man's sexual and ethical relations, passing over the pre-appropriable fecundity of the sexual encounter in favour of a fecundity that is sexually prescribed. Irigaray claims that Levinas inaugurates the fecundity of the caress as a masculine economy rather than the reminder given by each lover to the other of a profoundly intimate being-in-the-mother as the site of an impossible origin of the ethical.

Both Irigaray and Derrida observe that there is an unacknowledged assumption of sexual difference in Levinas's insistence on the primacy of ethics (otherness as wholly other, always already before sexual difference) over sexual difference (otherness as otherwise sexed, the other sex). Irigaray makes the point as follows: 'To become other to himself, to return to the other, Levinas needs the son. The son is his being as same/other, in a simultaneous engenderment that he seems to forget somewhat' (1991b: 110). Derrida makes the point in the form of a question: 'How can one mark as masculine the very thing said to be anterior, or even foreign, to sexual difference?' (1991b: 40). What both Irigaray and Derrida are asserting is that it is not possible to argue for the asexuality of ethical relations while specifying fecundity in (homo)sexual terms.

Asymmetrical subjectivity, which is the site of transcendence, is already conditioned by an exclusion in the form of sexual difference. In deconstructing Levinas's position, Derrida cites the prioritization of the human other over the sexed other in a commentary by Levinas on the Genesis story: 'Humanity cannot be thought beginning from two entirely different principles. There must be some *sameness* common to these *others*: woman has been chosen above man, but has come after him: the very femininity of woman consists in this initial afterwards.'[2]

Ethics is the necessary first principle in Levinas's account of humanity. Ethics is a relationship to an other which allows no other determination beyond otherness. This universal unconditionality would be compromised by any differentiation according to sex: 'It isn't woman who is secondary, it is the relation to woman *qua* woman that doesn't belong to the primordial human plan. What is primary are the tasks accomplished by man as a human being, and by woman as a human being.'[3] Levinas argues that woman, or the feminine, is not secondary to man, or the masculine, but rather the inauguration of difference, which is secondary to ethics. So the feminine is only secondary in its sexuate being, in so far as it is a relationship of sexual rather than ontological difference.

The problem which confronts Levinas here is that in the name of ethics he reinstates sexual neutrality in all its masculinity as the human paradigm. His solution, which in no way engages with this problem, is to maintain that humans are sexual beings, but their sexuality is secondary to a transcendental humanity. Furthermore his masterful answer is a violation of his own ethics. As Tina Chanter describes Derrida's question of Levinas, 'precisely in making sexual difference secondary, has [Levinas] not affirmed as neutral what is in fact masculine, has [Levinas] not mastered femininity by mastering its origin, sexual difference[?]' (Chanter, 1991: 143). Thus mastered, writes Derrida, femininity always falls back within the sphere of the same: 'Included in the same, it is by the same stroke excluded: enclosed within, foreclosed within the immanence of a crypt' (1991b: 43). Derrida reverses the significance of Levinas's naming of femininity as sexual difference, which rather than being a limit to ethics is 'always to make sexual difference secondary *as* femininity' (1991b: 43).

The question of the relationship between sexual difference and ethics in Levinas's work can be pursued further. While self-realization is ultimately a relationship of proximity between father and son, Levinas's account of femininity and maternity does not allow for the possibility of an ethical responsibility between mother and daughter as *sexed* beings – the feminine has no other, no face to face. There can be no encounter with the feminine face – Levinas's account of carnal intimacy revolves around feminine effacement; it does not refer to faces which kiss.[4] On the other hand, maternity is a being for the other divested of sexual difference. A consideration of the dynamic between maternity and the mother as woman is not possible in Levinas's account of ethical subjectivity, while paternity – in relationship to a son – is the fulfilment of man's erotic and metaphysical relations with the Other. In Levinas's terms the feminine is not a sexuate incarnation which I can share with others. It is not a nostalgia for an unmediated relation with the (m)other which is the issue here,[5] but rather that the effacement of the feminine precludes any such relations at all.

Tracing the various levels used by Levinas in his work, Irigaray questions why fecundity is an ontological category opening on to a metaphysical desire, while carnal intimacy is defined as a phenomenological relation. Carnal intimacy does not open on to a transcendental being or the other, but rather constitutes an interval of withdrawal from the phenomenality of being. Irigaray challenges Levinas for the way he chooses to employ these two different levels of discourse in his writing – both a metaphysical level, and a phenomenological level from which metaphysical entities have been detached (Irigaray, 1991b: 113). In choosing a phenomenological approach to describe the carnal relation, Levinas allows erotic love to fall within the constitution of the (one) subject in a universe of light. The alterity of the feminine is defined in relation to this ethical subjectivity, which realizes its responsibility through the feminine – through its donation, self-effacement and accommodation. The ethical is ultimately expressed in a social (face-to-face) as opposed to carnal interaction with the other. Invoking the figure of a female lover (*amante*) Irigaray rebukes Levinas for reducing the beloved to a passive femininity, which he turns from to claim his own infinity. Woman remains a being who is infantile and perverse, robbed of a chance of her own incarnation in order to grant man his.[6]

Irigaray considers that Levinas's privileging of paternity as the locus of ethical self-realization is a displacement of the genealogy of mother–daughter relationships. As far as she is concerned this displacement is symptomatic of the extent to which Levinas's phenomenology of the caress remains implicated in an ontotheological framework. In this ontotheology, the divine is a transcendent ego-ideal or the Other from which man is separated, while woman is without genre of her own, defined negatively as man's material other, or alter ego.[7] There can be no sense of transcendence in an act reserved for man's animal nature, as an existence which he desires to overcome. Levinas's conception of sexual difference is set within the context of a suprasensory god who has withdrawn from the act of carnal love. Nothing of this monotheistic god is accessible to the senses – he can be grasped only in invisible form (Irigaray, 1991b: 117).

Against an ontotheological configuration of love and desire which renders both gods and women more invisible than night, in her statements about the irreducibility of one sex to the other Irigaray is emphasizing that each sex is not entirely incorporable by the other; *between* the sexes, there is always a material remainder.[8] This remainder is the limitation within which Irigaray contends that there can be sexuate existence, compared with the anonymous materiality of existence which Levinas proposes: '[t]he *there is* remains a present that may be subject to pressure by the god, but it does not form a foundation for the triumph of sexual fecundity' (Irigaray, 1993a: 14). The point of the non-substitutibility of the sexuate other for Irigaray is that sexual difference is the mark of the impossibility of determining the alterity of the other.

A light of no account

Irigaray begins her reading of Levinas's phenomenology of Eros with her own description of erotic pleasure, which she describes as a pleasure taken by sensuality in its beginning. This is not an archaeological or a 'new age' conception of eroticism; it is not a rediscovery or re-enactment of an original birth. Nor is it a reproductively conceived birth. Erotic pleasure is an imaginary beginning, a birth after and before the present which will never have taken place. Voluptuousness undoes all schemas, all thematization of the world. It is a beginning without memory, a beginning which knows no other. In contrast to conscious motivation, erotic pleasure is an acceptance of that which gives of itself, of that which is of no account, of that which has not yet come into being. It has no basis in the subject that sees things, but is still carnal – a state of immersion, a being lost in the 'sensual pleasure of birth into a world where the look itself remains tactile – open to the light' (Irigaray, 1993a: 185).

A well-known feature of Irigaray's work is her association of eroticism with the affect of wonder rather than a relation that is inadequate to language. Wonder is the feeling that erupts in the face of the absolutely other. In her reading of Descartes' *Meditations*, Irigaray reiterates his naming of wonder as the first of the passions:

> Wonder is not an enveloping. It corresponds to time, to space-time before and after that which can delimit, go round, encircle. It constitutes an

113

opening prior to and following that which surrounds, enlaces. It is the passion of that which is already born and not yet re-enveloped in love. Of that which is touched and moves toward and within the attraction, without nostalgia for the first dwelling. Outside of repetition. It is the passion of the first encounter. And of perpetual rebirth? An affect that would subsist among all forms of others irreducible each to the other. The passion that inaugurates love and art. And thought.

(Irigaray, 1993a: 81–2)

Irigaray refers to the touching in wonder as the touch of the caress. The caress is not so much a touch as it is the gesture of touch, an alternation between movement and posture, simultaneously dissolving and constituting itself without memory or distinction. This gesture is a never-to-be-grasped beginning, an attraction without consummation, always on the threshold of appetite, not yet anticipating or yearning an other. The caress affirms and protects its infinite otherness in the prolongation of a birth which will never come to pass. Untouched by mastery, it is before and beyond any subject or setting. Life, made familiar in its consumption and habitation, is suspended and reopened in the gesture of the caress.

For Irigaray, the caress is the most elementary gesture of fecundity. She links this gesture, attentive to the regeneration and renewal of life, with a love that is given over to a night in whose elemental indivisibility there is a future 'where things have not yet taken their places but remain possible' (1993a: 197). Levinas concentrates on the withdrawal of the feminine from signification in his phenomenology of the caress. Eroticism is a movement away from light, beyond conscious discrimination, a dissolution of incarnation into an unsignifiable carnality. Irigaray, however, regards the caress as an incomparable sense of incarnation, as a gesture prolonging its incompletion. Rather than a diffusion of formal identity which is sought out in the elusiveness of touch, Irigaray conceives of the caress as a participation in the transmutability of flesh. This conception is not set against Levinas's text but, instead, extends the significance of touch in a way which he does not consider.

Irigaray is not alone in rereading the significance of touch in Levinas's work which emphasizes its unique relationship to incarnation. Edith Wyschogrod, for example, considers touch within the phenomenological premise that the subject in the world is based on a corporeality which eludes observation, yet is the principle through which the world appears (Wyschogrod, 1980). In terms of Levinas's theory of proximity, touch becomes the body's vulnerability to the

114

impingement of the world. In Wyschogrod's formulation, touch escapes any general theory of sensation. Instead, tactility is a generic sensibility which constitutes the opposition of interiority and exteriority.

Wyschogrod goes so far as to insist that the tactile is not a sense at all. The body positioned by touch is not manifest in consciousness. Anterior to and underlying all sensation, tactility is the actualization of the subject as a singling out of the body in proximity with the given. Founded upon tactility, interiority is defined as that which remains inaccessible to contact. Touching does not incorporate the body into the world as a whole. It is an exposition based on a disruption of context. Wyschogrod refers to 'being touched' as a 'being moved', a comportment of the body which requires the abandonment of a previous schema. The motility of the body points to the contingency of totality, rather than the unified totality of an overriding consciousness. The importance of tactility is that, before any conscious determination of one's being in the world, touching is a way of actualizing or taking up a position without reference to any schema or telos, without beginning by way of the possible. Devoid of reference to any locatable origin, touching is the condition of possibility of ritual transfigurations rather than conscious acts.

Irigaray describes the tactile as the most archaic and subtle mode of perception. Touching abides by a contact which does not dissolve or remember borders but seeks a perpetual reaffirmation of palpable flesh. Touch is the sense which underlines all others, and the sense which forgets and reconstitutes itself in the moment of touching:

> Before orality comes to be, touch is already in existence. No nourishment can compensate for the grace or work of touching. Touch makes it possible to wait, to gather strength, so that the other will return to caress and reshape, from within and from without, a flesh that is given back to itself in the gesture of love. The most subtly necessary guardian of my life is the other's flesh.

> (Irigaray, 1993a: 187)

Irigaray describes the mode of touching in the caress as an encounter in which all desire of imposing an identity on the in-stance is sacrificed to remaining perpetually on the threshold of its attraction. In Irigaray's account of the caress incarnation is an indefinite instantiation or opening within the language of being. Voluptuousness is an abandonment of the familiar, a staking of life in the affirmation of an otherness that will never be manifest to consciousness.

Levinas describes this as a movement away from the light. Aligned on the side of the self in its carnality, rather than a subjectivity in its own right, the feminine represents the limits of phenomenal subjectivity in the body's materiality. Levinas theorizes eroticism as a passion for an other whose materiality is inadequate to and transcends meaningful exchange. The mastery of light is not a feminine vocation. Within this schema the feminine embodies a descent into carnality and, accompanying this, a loss of visibility. Irigaray takes this movement further. Voluptuousness is a re-turning to a state of movement, a corporeality oscillating between matter and light. Far from simply being a movement into night, this is a passion for an unopposable, unknowable, unfixable light. Levinas calls the wonder of light which Plato put at the origin of philosophy 'an astonishment before the natural and the intelligible' (1978a: 22). In Levinas's own account, light's intelligibility is related to the subject. Irigaray is more interested in considering illumination as a passion, as a first and inexhaustible love.[9] Wonder is not only an astonishment by light, but a perpetual movement, an opening up to light within the immobilization of sight. The sheer novelty of light, and not the clarity of knowledge, is what animates the thoughts of the philosophers. For Descartes it is a passion for a light which, free of an object, rejuvenates the brain (Irigaray, 1993a: 80).

For Irigaray illumination is a never-to-be-grasped carnal beginning, a beginning without which there can be no emergence of life out of chaos and formlessness. Illumination is 'that less-than-nothing which is not nothing – light' (1993a: 197). Illumination is an encounter of wonder, an encounter born of a carnality which cannot be apprehended. This wonder is a source of animation – a movement in one's being, not of any lasting impression. It is an opening up to light which brings nothing into relief, conveys no sense of things, is unfixable and unopposable. It is an opening of affection. Prior to any vision, the movement of illumination is a (re-)exposition of flesh that precedes any ordering of and incorporation into a world.

Irigaray's conception of love differs from Levinas's theorization of love as a desire for the abyss. The abandonment of the loving gesture is not simply a quitting of the status of existent but, for the woman lover as much as a man, an acceding to the caress. The depth of night to which Levinas refers in his phenomenology of Eros is described by Irigaray as a place to which the woman lover returns, to which she allows herself to sink. The primordiality of this depth must be distinguished from the concept of depth as 'bathos' which refers to a geometrical depth of already formed material things. Irigaray conceives of depth as an immersion in a medium whose density is not nothing, without which it is not possible to conceive of things.[10] For Irigaray, lovers negotiate the chiasm which together they become, entrusting between them in their exchange of love that they will each be delivered separately into the world:

> . . . surpassing the corruption of what has already been seen. Return to a certain night whence the lovers can arise differently illuminated and enlightened. They give themselves to each other and give up what has already been made. Of themselves and of reason. Opening to an innocence that runs the risk of folding back on itself in defense of the past. In this gesture each one runs the risk of annihilating, killing, or rescuscitating.
>
> (Irigaray, 1993a: 193)

Against Levinas's depiction of consciousness's enthralment with an unsignifiable materiality, Irigaray invokes a materiality that resists static identification in the erotic embrace. Irigaray maintains that Levinas confines the feminine to an unchanging interval in his account of love, abandoning the beloved to a non-existent dwelling in an unlit and infantile place. The beloved disappears into the anonymity of flesh, as a non-human animality in the night. While the caress is the threshold of his fecundity, it is the exhaustion of hers in an extravagant carnality that will never dwell in the light of day.

In his phenomenology of night Levinas turns from the sun in search of a nocturnal, powerless source of light, while the trajectory of his ethics can be characterized as a dream of passing beyond light. Derrida describes Levinas's conception of erotic light as an anarchic light:

> A community of non-presence, and therefore of non-phenomenality. Not a community without light . . . but a community anterior to Platonic light. A light before neutral light, before the truth which arrives as a third party, the truth 'which we look toward together'.
>
> (1978: 91)

Levinas proposes a light of discursivity that lends nothing to visibility beyond resistance to disclosure, and is before and beyond the light of reason. As well as a similarity between Irigaray and Levinas in their proposal of a light that subverts identity[11] Irigaray also emphasizes the extent to which Levinas's account of the caress remains within a phenomenological paradigm which falls short of an erotic light. Irigaray's conception of a light before Platonic light does not take her into the night of non-phenomenality, but to a philosophy of the elemental, a philosophy before and after Platonic light. I would describe Irigaray's conception of the non-disclosure of erotic light as a photosensitivity or exposure to alterity in the erotic encounter, rather than a light that illuminates reason or nature or god.[12] A factor in Irigaray's formulation that works against the trajectory of Levinas's ethics is that erotic light is unsurpassable, unopposable. For Irigaray, the caress is 'an ecstasy that remains *in-stant*', or a re-turning with/in the self (1993a: 14).[13] It is a beginning which is materially conceived. There is no means of transcending this erotic beginning. In remaining on the threshold of the instance it will never have come to pass.

Levinas limits his experience of erotic love to the phenomenology of the caress. In her study of Levinas and also in her theorizing of the elemental, Irigaray invokes the uncontainability of orgasmic flesh:

> Luminous night, touched with a quickening whose denseness never appears in the light. Neither permanently fixed, nor shifting and fickle. Nothing solid survives, yet that thickness responding to its own rhythms is not nothing. Quickening in movements both expected and unexpected. Your space, your time are unable to grasp their regularity or contain their foldings and unfoldings. The force unleashed has an intensity which cannot be anywhere measured, nor contained.
>
> (Irigaray, 1992: 13)

The sexual encounter is not, as Levinas theorizes, a lapse in presence, but a reminder of flesh which resembles no other. Irigaray reverses the order of fecundity and conception, claiming that without fecundity there can be no conception. What is shaped in the caress is a place of commencement which cannot be assumed, without schema or telos or anticipation of presence.

Irigaray continues Levinas's analysis of the caress beyond the point where consciousness resigns when it loses all sense of relation to the other. Irigaray takes this relation up as one of wonder, in the unforeseeable nature of exposure to otherness: 'Wonder would be the passion of the most material and the most metaphysical, of their possible conception and fecundation one by the other. A third dimension. An intermediary. Neither the one nor the other. Which is not to say neutral or neuter' (1993a: 82). Irigaray describes the encounter of wonder as a sensitivity which brings nothing into relief, provides no outlines or resistance, but moves with impulsion, intensity, energy, colour and rhythm, devoid of the separation of night and light.

While Levinas associates a turning from light in eroticism with the loss of self and a descent into an unsignifiable carnality, Irigaray conceives of eroticism as the incomparable night of lovers absorbed in prolonging the threshold of illumination. In adhering to an unforeseeable sensitivity to light Irigaray articulates the issue of woman's exclusion from her act in the caress – an act which according to Levinas never takes place. Irigaray regards the caress as the fecund threshold in which each sex can establish a chiasm which allows movement between self and other to take place (1993a: 9). As agent of the caress woman takes on the envelope of her own desire and assumes the material garb of her own self, entrusting her formation to nothing other than her fidelity to flesh.

Part IV

EROTIC LIGHT

10

Conclusion

In Irigaray's rereading of Levinas's 'Phenomenology of Eros' the flesh illuminated in the caress has no basis in the body as either a concept or a thing sustainable within the parameters of embodiment which the sensible/intelligible binarism of photology has upheld in its varying historical forms. Like Merleau-Ponty's account of 'lighting' and Levinas's proposition of a discursive light rather than a light of disclosure, wonder is illumination as an animating encounter that intervenes in this photological discourse. Irigaray's elaboration of the linkage between photology and masculine identity in *Speculum* is widely known. In concluding I will outline some features of an erotic light that can be drawn from Irigaray's work which can be characterized as the giving/acceding of form in an inexhaustible movement of disappropriation or unmastering of the logic of this isomorphism.

The illumination of flesh in the caress is not an embodied ideality or the preconceivable first light of consciousness, but is a (re)generation in the body. In this respect Bataille's sustained eroticization of light stands as an important precedent to Irigaray's work. Bataille taunts the eye of detached vision with the toxic light of its own erotic waste, from the carnal excesses of *lumen naturale* to the searing excrements of the sun.[1] His unconditional rejection of the metaphor of an illuminating sun is a move which has resonances in Irigaray's analyses of mysticism and Plato's *Hystera* in *Speculum*, although her critical project is located more within a utopian than an Icarian topos in relation to the sun.[2] The emphasis in Bataille's writing falls on the dissolution of intelligible vision in the incalculable profligacy of eroticism. In stark contrast to Merleau-Ponty's account of the ideality of light originating in flesh, Bataille strips away any fantasy of the conditional intelligibility of carnally constituted light and exposes the grotesqueness of the illumination which lies at the basis of humanity's highest strivings.

Instead of a noble state of communion with the infinite through the mediation of light, Bataille describes the couplings of sight as a wanton excessiveness which resists idealization in any form. The extent of Bataille's inversion of the source of Descartes' *lumen naturale* is expressed by Jay:

> The enucleated eye was a parodic version of the separation of sight from the body characteristic of the Cartesian tradition; no longer able to see, it was thrust back into the body through vaginal orifices in ways that mocked in advance Merleau-Ponty's benign reembodiment of the eye in the 'flesh of the world'.
>
> (Jay, 1993a: 220)

For Bataille, horror is a preferable means of breaking the hold of photology's appropriation of vision, and returning to the carnal source of light: 'it alone is brutal enough to break everything that stifles'.[3] By way of comparison, Irigaray resists the association of the diffusion of formal identity in the profligacy of eroticism with the non-negatable nothingness of horror. Horror exposes matter as an exorbitance which disrupts form. However, left exposed as such, horror also perpetuates the fate of matter as eternal supplement to incarnation or, as Irigaray discusses in 'La Mysterique', a bride whose only value is to be wasted (1985a: 193). Instead of horror, the emphasis in Irigaray's work falls on the caress as an unconditional transcendental giving of carnality in the re-memoration of matter.

For Irigaray the caress is a gesture that both touches on and differs from the gesture of maternity. It speaks of a regeneration in the body that is other than the maternal body of sexual reproduction. At the heart of that reproductive discourse is the mythology of an immutable form of engendering in which matter remains the inconceivable site and receptacle for the reproduction of intelligible form. Levinas remains within a reproductive paradigm in so far as he limits the fecundity of the body of beloved to sexual fecundity in his phenomenology of the caress. In his account of ethical subjectivity the manner in which Levinas differentiates between phenomenological light and a discursive light serves to reiterate the displacement of an erotic as opposed to patrilineally based generation in the body. He extends his account of discursive light only to the expression of the transcendent singularity of the human other. The feminine other remains the inexpressible embodiment of alterity in her evasion of formal disclosure.

124

Irigaray avoids any idea of generation in the body that reproduces a view of matter that is aligned with the feminine in its photological conception. To adopt such a position would be to remain within the modern heliocentrism of atomic light. Atomic physics is generally credited with uncovering the sun residing at the core of every atom of matter. Woman occupies a place in the atomic paradigm as a negativity which circulates towards but never returns to herself as a locus of development of a positive form. Her relation to being takes a trajectory synonymous with the electron, perpetually in motion, ever diverging, never in touch with itself, lacking a proper place: 'In terms of contemporary physics, it could be said that she remains on the side of the electron, with all that this implies for her, for man, for their encounter' (Irigaray, 1993a: 9). This movement is most explicitly demonstrated by Levinas in his confining of the beloved to a situation in which she radiates an erotic light as she gives up her existence.

The atomic notion of the disclosure of presence is based on the transformation of matter into light energy.[4] In Irigaray's hands, dis-closure is both a perpetual opening and a communicative gesture. Rather than a movement that is related to the assurance of an ideal presence, Irigaray capitalizes on the unprecedented potential for the destruction of matter contained within this atomic schema. Arguing against the fixation of sexual difference as a formal distinction that upholds the ideal of a singular subjectivity, she reworks the idea of generative matter into a site of an unidentifiable unmasterable threshold that is perpetuated in the erotic gesture. This is an indiscriminate dis-closure or photosensitivity which does not reproduce any formless 'outside'. In place of a femininity that lacks an identity in an atomized subjective schema Irigaray considers that both positive and negative poles of intentionality must be present in each sex and that their different subjective positions must be negotiated between them together: 'What is missing is the double pole of attraction and support, which excludes disintegration or rejection, attraction and decomposition, but which instead ensures the separation that articulates every encounter and makes possible speech, promises, alliances' (1993a: 9).

As an illumination that remains in-stant, erotic light represents a break with an ex-static presence, or the dream of a being able to go beyond itself which Levinas reworks in his ethical characterization of an absolute future that is 'not yet' establishable in the light of the present. Irigaray's position varies from the critical position that Levinas takes in relation to Heidegger's idea of existence as a movement of the present projecting a future.[5] For Levinas the stance of the subject is the movement of an instance understood not as a limit, but as a present interruptive event (see Llewellyn, 1995: 27). For Irigaray the caress is the renewal of being-in-momentum in an ex-stasy that is in-stant.

Unlike Merleau-Ponty's subject/object body that exists in the co-extensivity of an exteriority and interiority folded within itself, the in-stance which Irigaray refers to is an interiority that cannot be thought in terms of the intertwining of subject and object. In contrast to Merleau-Ponty's use of the idea of touching oneself as the most elementary way in which a subject–predicate distinction begins to be established, Irigaray argues that in touching oneself what or who is subject and what or who is object will never be known because neither of these positions can be distinguished from the other. As Irigaray makes much of in the 'two lips', the doubling and positioning of the self in relation to the self in its sensible immediacy is figured as an impossibility within the limits of the self conceived of as a unified phenomenon.

In this sense the mobile differentiation of the tactile body preconditions the eye as an organ of vision and is the basis upon which touch cannot be subordinated to vision, although the means by which they are related vitally concerns Irigaray. Nor is vision like touch, which is the most elementary sense of animate being or (re)incarnation. Irigaray regards tactility as the primordial sense in which the body's interiority is constituted, or the first sense in which we constitute a living space or opening within the self. The caress gives shape to flesh in the form of a non-negatable, non-incorporable otherness as the site of an affection that cannot be gathered. However, rather than some inchoate matter that is set in motion in being passed from hand to hand, there is no self determining the instance of an affection which defies the play of similitude and is never experienced as either an idea or a thing. This unidentifiable imaginary reserve which is perpetuated in touch is an interiority or site of initiation of a corporeality that must be constantly negotiated.

Taken on its own this account of touch risks the charge of a genetic formulation. By way of contrast the reduction of contact in contemporary technologies to an interval that occurs at the speed of light is an example of a texture of light that has collapsed touch and vision. As Paul Virilio comments, the constant character of light's absolute speed now conditions our phenomenal apperception of the world's duration and extension, or our experience of time and space. As digitization establishes the means for translating and reintegrating the senses,[6] the immobilizing effects of the apparent obliteration of an unidentifiable site of material passage become evident. In Virilio's discussion of the instant of electro-optical, electro-acoustic and electro-tactile tele-technologies as a present that takes place in no space/time at all he observes a new form of stasis: 'note the similarities that now exist between the reduced mobility of the equipped invalid and the growing inertia of the overequipped, "valid" human population' (Virilio, 1993: 12). A significant feature of speed as a critical transition is that, in severing the tangible instantiation of the body from the body as a discrete transmissible telepresence, its translatability or capacity for transformation from one state into another is reduced to a dimensionless, atomized motility.

Irigaray contrasts the liminal flesh of the contiguously formed interiority of the tangible invisible with the cave or vessel-like inhabitable morphology of traditional femininity. In and of itself the tangible invisible does not represent an alternative recognizable feminine morphology. Becoming a woman cannot be established on the basis of a subjective immediacy. For Irigaray the dividedness of existence cannot be read reflexively in the case of woman, since there is no property of woman in existence. Instead Irigaray maintains that each being of woman differs in relation with itself such that no gathering of the difference is possible. Before the intentionality of the 'double touch' (which divides touch between sentient being and the touched object), the indeterminacy of the 'hands that touch without taking hold – like the lips' (1993a: 170) constitutes the body as a threshold, neither as a perceived interior nor outside surface, but as 'the passage . . . between . . .' (1993a: 170).

The significance of feminine indeterminacy as it is formulated in the 'two lips' is not that it valorizes a feminine multiplicity. Rather, given that the division of subject–object is not a determination that woman is party to, it calls for thought to be given about ways in which becoming a woman is not a simple projectable objective nor an ideal that is unimplicated in traditional representations determined by unity, self-sameness and identity. Feminine being is an impossibility in so far as a subjectivity that knows nothing of itself as an object cannot properly be a subjectivity.[7] Without an objective orientation woman's relation to being remains an affective immediacy somewhere between an instinct and an intentionality that has no object. While woman is able to have feelings and take pleasure in herself, without being able to view these feelings in a field of intentionality or as an objective (not as a fixed objective, but a moving in relation to) she is unable to have any knowledge of a feminine sexual dimension in eroticism, love, ethics, or spirit. The problem is not simply one of ethical responsibility in relation to formalization, as Levinas proposes in his critique of the subject of light. It is also, and inseparably linked to this, the problem of an identity that resists formalization.

The tangible invisible is a tactile imaginary that poses itself as a problem of translation or transformation of identity into a style which is not based on a formal structure (Irigaray, 1993a: 171). It is instead the incalculable limit of a being that is constantly taking form, or turning to life in the gesture of giving way. It is not my intention to draw from this a unique or private feminine space in terms of a tactile imaginary, which would be to settle for a prescriptive formulation of feminine identity. Rather, if our desires, aspirations and ethical concerns as women are to be 'seen' politically it is necessary actively to intervene in the history of light and in turn to violate the texture in which woman has been rendered a figure of invisibility and left without means of negotiating any objective perspective on the situatedness of her sensible being. Erotic light exposes that objective as the persistent and discomforting issue of the impossibility of seeing identically in different worlds, while challenging any attempt to view the world in a neutral light that erases all traces of sexual difference.

Notes

1 Introduction

1 The distinction between visible and invisible light, also known as 'lux' and 'lumen', is an ancient and ambiguous one. 'Lumen' refers to the physical movement of invisible rays of light whose perfect linearity is the essence of illumination and requires no organ of sight. The passage of lumen is transparent and imperceivable. On the other hand, 'lux' refers to the phenomenon of light, or light as it is experienced in sight, composed of colour, shadow and visible qualities. Generally speaking lux is the subjective experience of light. Vasco Ronchi gives an outline of the fate of these terms in the history of optics (Ronchi, 1957: 3–23). See also Ronchi (1970) for an historical study of light conceived of as having physical, physiological and psychological phases.

2 This dichotomy between visible and invisible light has been reconstituted hierarchically in many different ways by theologians, philosophers, artists and scientists alike. Broadly defined, invisible light is the light of ideas, speculation, inference, revelation and divine illumination, and visible light is the light of facticity, observation, discovery, empirical evidence and knowledge. While different philosophical traditions have valorized one form of light over the other, both have the common effect of linking truth and vision. Martin Jay observes that one of the most powerful sources of ocularcentrism or the privileging of vision in the West has been the certainty provided by the opposite term whenever the superiority of either has been discredited (Jay, 1993b: 105–6). The increasing complexity of the terms lux and lumen became a source of irresolvable confusion over time; and in contemporary physics, for example, visible and invisible light have been merged into the continuum of frequencies of the one electromagnetic spectrum. As modern languages replaced Latin, both terms were replaced by the single term *luce* (Italian), *light* (English), *lumière* (French), *luz* (Spanish) and *Licht* (German) (Ronchi 1957: 17–18). For an historical mapping of the complexities of the lux/lumen dualism, see Jay (1993a: 21–82).

3 See *The Republic* Part VII (Plato, 1955: 316–25).

4 Here also lies the tension between the Greek and Judaic intellectual traditions. Susan Handelman makes a connection between the metaphoric separation of truth and language, and the subordination of the Jewish Rabbinic tradition. The original unity of discourse and truth in Hebrew thinking was the very thing which the Greek Enlightenment disrupted. The Rabbinic aurally based attentiveness to the word is not concerned with the truth of representation, but with the interpretation of the true word (Handelman, 1982: 4).

5 'Meditations on First Philosophy', in *The Philosophical Works of Descartes* Vol. 1 (Descartes, 1931: 177).

6 Martin Jay discusses the extent to which Descartes failed, as he himself admitted, to describe adequately this relationship between lux and lumen (Jay, 1993a: 73–9).

7 See Martin Heidegger's discussion of these concepts generally in 'The Origin of the Work of Art', 'Letter on Humanism', 'The Question Concerning Technology', and 'The End of Philosophy and the Task of Thinking', in *Basic Writings* (Heidegger, 1977a).

8 Blumenberg emphasizes the Latin root of this term, *intueri* (to gaze upon), differentiating it from the contemporary sense of intuition as non-rational perception (Blumenberg, 1993: 54fn).

9 See 'White Mythology: Metaphor in the Text of Philosophy', in *Margins of Philosophy* (Derrida, 1982: 207–71).

10 See 'Plato's Pharmacy', in *Dissemination* (Derrida, 1981a: 75–84).

11 See 'The Question Concerning Technology', in *The Question Concerning Technology and Other Essays* (Heidegger, 1977b: 20).

12 'Metaphor, therefore, is determined by philosophy as a provisional loss of meaning, an economy of the proper without irreparable damage, a certainly inevitable detour, but also a history with its sights set on, and within the horizon of, the circular reappropriation of literal, proper meaning' (Derrida, 1982: 270).

13 By way of example, it is this allowance that is foregrounded in twentieth-century architectural figurations of windows as a passage which 'gives light'. See Thomas Keenan (1993: 121–41).

14 See '*Khōra*', in *On the Name* (Derrida, 1995: 89–127).

15 Zoe Sofoulis draws attention to the corporeal basis of the metaphor of illumination, invoking a play on 'lumen' as further explication of the 'forgotten' vagina of which Irigaray speaks. As Sofoulis explains, in physics a 'lumen' is a unit of light flux. In anatomy, Sofoulis observes, the term is used to describe bodily cavities and spaces, such as those of blood vessels, glandular orifices or the cytoplasm within cell walls. Here light is extended to mean both light-space and cavity or hole. Within this double sense, or play of similitude between space and lumen, light can be thought of as space, and space as light. Displacing the material means by which it achieves its metaphoric basis, light takes on the feminine aspect of a vacant matrix. In this light, which is of heliotropic origin, man ultimately finds a unique dwelling, or space which is his own (Sofoulis, 1988: 280–300).

As well as expanding upon Irigaray's reading of heliocentrism, Sofoulis regards Irigaray's omission of the association between 'lumen' and the 'forgotten vagina' as a missed opportunity. She argues that Irigaray's preoccupations with the idea of the cave as *hystera* (womb) and with the logic of light (photology) could be directed to an explication of 'lumen' which would further identify the corporeal basis of heliocentrism in its various historical forms. Sofoulis herself extends this theme to the light of a luminary body in the solar system – the moon. Any equation of reason with sunlight is made by way of this intermediary lunar term, meaning, Sofoulis argues, that photology requires more than one body. The moon is the paradigm of tropism or half-light. Standing closer to the sun, and deflecting its blinding rays: 'The moon would be an exemplar of an intermediary between the "primitive proper sense" of the sensible sun and its re-originated "figurative sense" of the light of reason' (Sofoulis, 1988: 280). As Sofoulis argues, Irigaray does not direct her attention to an explication of the corporeality of light in her discussion of Plato's *Hystera*. I suggest, however, that to do so in the context of heliocentrism would be to risk associating corporeality with a notion of fixed bodies of a solar system.

16 I borrow this progression from Margaret Whitford (1991a: 108–9).

17 For an outline of the imaginary body and its politico-cultural implications see Moira Gatens (1991: 115–18). The theme is discussed at length in her *Imaginary Bodies: Ethics, Power and Corporeality* (1996).

18 See, for example, Susan Stewart's study of this crisis (1993).

19 See, for example, *The Tain of the Mirror: Derrida and the Philosophy of Reflection* (Gasché, 1986).

20 For an interpretation of Irigaray's analysis of Plato's *Hystera* as a refocusing of the powers of philosophy's metaphoric sun, see Philippa Berry (1994: 229–46).

21 See, for example, Hans Jonas's essay 'The Nobility of Sight', where discussion of the valorization of sight is based on the extent to which vision gives a sense of an immaterial and thus infinite object (Jonas, 1954: 507–19).

22 There are currently two published English translations of Irigaray's essay on Levinas. The first translation, by Alphonso Lingis, is published in *Face to Face with Levinas* (Cohen, 1986: 231–56).

23 Psychoanalysis itself was condemned on the grounds of its visual emphasis. Hélène Cixous, for example, called it 'a voyeur's theory' (Cixous, 1980: 95).

24 Jay is referring here principally to Alice A. Jardine's criticism of the adherence of feminism to deconstruction (Jardine, 1985). Of the many other critics who also address this issue, Gayatri Chakravorty Spivak has undertaken the most comprehensive interrogation (Spivak, 1983: 169–95; 1987: 134–53; 1989: 206–23).

25 For example, in relation to Irigaray's theorizing of gender asymmetry in general as a consequence of a monological discourse, Judith Butler asks: 'Is it possible to identify a monolithic as well as a monologic masculinist economy that traverses the array of cultural and historical contexts in which sexual difference takes place?' (Butler, 1990: 13).

26 Jay quotes Irigaray from an interview in *Les Femmes, la pornographie et l'érotisme*, eds Marie Françoise Hans and Gilles Lapouge (Paris, 1978), p. 50 (Jay, 1993a: 493).

27 'Because in relation to the working of theory, the/a woman fulfills a twofold function – as the mute outside that sustains all systematicity; as a maternal and still silent ground that nourishes all foundations – she does not have to conform to the codes theory has set up for itself. In this way, she confounds, once again, the imaginary of the "subject" – in its masculine connotations – and something that will or might be the imaginary of the female' (Irigaray, 1985a: 365).

28 See 'The Three Genders', in *Sexes and Genealogies* (Irigaray, 1993b: 177).

29 In his turn Derrida is open to Irigaray's criticism that he 'masters' the identity of 'woman' as nothing but a trope for the undecidability of meaning.

30 Irigaray is aligned with anti-visual thought in a different way by Andrea Nye (1993). In an essay which is devoted to Irigaray's critique of speculative metaphysics she is positioned as an anti-visual theorist because of her philosophical alliances. Irigaray is caught, Nye proposes, within the negativity of the metaphysics which she attempts to abandon. Nye's essay positions Irigaray as a theorist who is detached from living vision. Nye focuses on Irigaray's concern with metaphysics and her demonstration that the history of philosophy is the repetition of an isomorphic imaginary. She argues that in Irigaray's determination to cast philosophy as a psychical drama in eternal synchrony with itself she leaves us with an image of an ageless youth. By way of contrast, Nye portrays Wittgenstein's photo-logicism as the last gasp of metaphysical vision with all its flesh withered away, 'finally detached from any reference to physical things'. As an argument against a totalizing view of philosophy, Nye's point has a validity which is consistent with Irigaray's own attempts to pass through the philosopher's mirror of resemblances. But it is difficult to argue that Irigaray's project is in synchrony with the logic of metaphysical vision when Irigaray herself regards ocularcentrism as an anti-visual chronicle full of blind spots, mirror vision and the eyes of recently dead men. Nye's essay represents Irigaray as a midwife, who with a singularity of vision assists a philosophical system with its self-birth metaphors. She takes issue with Irigaray for recasting metaphysics in psychoanalytic terms when Irigaray herself gives sufficient indication in the text of *Speculum* that there are many other versions of early Greek life which she might have used to dispel the Platonic myth. What if, Nye suggests, Irigaray had considered the everyday social interactions of those Greeks, who would not have lived their lives with their eyes focused on eternity, let alone with such monocular and insecure vision? However, to argue that Irigaray should attend to the real and not the metaphoric vision of the Greeks is to adhere to the logic of resemblance and to return there for its (re-)origination.

2 Introduction to Merleau-Ponty

1 For a general discussion of Merleau-Ponty's philosophy in relation to Hegel, Heidegger and Lacan, as well as Husserl, see Mark Taylor (1987: 61–81).

2 Bernard Charles Flynn characterizes Merleau-Ponty's non-oppositional approach to consciousness in Derridean terms, as a departure from the opposition between the

sensible and the intelligible (the visible and the invisible), or as a break with one of the founding gestures of metaphysics (Flynn, 1984: 164–79).

3 'It is already the flesh of things that speaks to us of our own flesh, and that speaks to us of the flesh of the other—My "look" is one of those givens of the "sensible," of the brute and primordial world, that defies the analysis into being and nothingness, into existence as consciousness and existence as a thing, and requires a complete reconstruction of philosophy' (Merleau-Ponty, 1968: 193).

4 See 'Meaning and Sense', in *Collected Philosophical Papers* (Levinas, 1987a: 75–80).

5 Michel Foucault's work in particular is deeply influenced by as well as critically opposed to Merleau-Ponty's notion of lived embodiment. Hubert L. Dreyfus and Paul Rabinow discuss the relationship between the two thinkers at length in *Michel Foucault: Beyond Structuralism and Hermeneutics* (1982). English-speaking theorists who have developed productive theoretic positions partially through both critical and sympathetic interpretations of Merleau-Ponty's account of lived embodiment include Alphonso Lingis (1985); Iris Marion Young (1990); Vivian Sobchack (1992); Jeffner Allen (1982–3); Judith Butler (1989; 1993); and Elizabeth Grosz (1993; 1994).

3 Living flesh

1 For a description of flesh in these terms see Gary Brent Madison (1990: 27–34).

2 Merleau-Ponty's observation refutes a notion of the body as subject as much as it refutes a notion of a transcendental subject. M. C. Dillon comments that in the secondary literature critics commonly misrepresent Merleau-Ponty's notion of the lived body in his later work by equating it with Kant's transcendental unity of apperception. He comments that, if anything, Merleau-Ponty is taking issue with Husserl's transcendentalism (Dillon, 1990: 14–26).

3 An example which Emmanuel Levinas uses to make the point about the implication of body and mind as flesh is that the 'mental gait' is also a movement of the human body (Levinas, 1990a: 61).

4 See 'Eye and Mind', in *The Primacy of Perception and Other Essays* (Merleau-Ponty, 1964a: 159–90). See also 'Cézanne's Doubt', in *Sense and Non-Sense* (Merleau-Ponty, 1964b: 9–25). Jacques Lacan comments extensively on Merleau-Ponty's account of painting in *The Four Fundamental Concepts of Psychoanalysis* (Lacan, 1979). For a discussion of Merleau-Ponty's conception of the dimensionality of the visible in painting see James Gordon Place (1976: 75–91) and Edward S. Casey (1991: 1–29).

5 Véronique M. Fóti describes Merleau-Ponty's understanding of dimensionality as ideality in relation to colour. Ideality cannot be severed from the sensory domain, but is, as Merleau-Ponty argues, sensibility's means of articulation (Fóti, 1990: 13–28).

6 I am grateful to Professor Anne Sefton of the Department of Physiology, University of Sydney, for outlining for me the technical and historical aspects of the physiology of vision which I have developed here, and in particular Peter Bishop's experimentation with artificial stereopsis. I would add by way of a historical aside that since Merleau-Ponty's death physiological interest in visual perception has shifted from

the effects of the optic chiasma to parallel processing of retinal stimuli in the brain. Parallel processing refers to the discovery that individual retinal cells do not simply respond to light in terms of presence/absence, but that different aspects of visual perception are registered separately in the field of the visual cortex corresponding to each retinal cell. In other words, interest in the physiology of vision has shifted to mapping a multi-dimensional visual field based on the lateral connections of the brain.

7 See 'The Double Session', in *Dissemination* (Derrida, 1981a: 173–286).

8 This is a spoken comment made by Derrida, which is related by Nancy J. Holland (1986: 111).

9 Bernard Charles Flynn discusses Derrida's statement: 'I don't know what perception is and I don't believe that anything like perception exists' (Flynn, 1984: 164).

10 The mother is represented as a *passive* participant in the moment of giving birth, that is, 'about to be delivered' of her baby.

11 Derrida explains his controversial position as follows: 'One could say quite accurately that the hymen *does not exist*. Anything constituting the value of existence is foreign to the "hymen". And if there were hymen – I am not saying if the hymen existed – property value would be no more appropriate to it for reasons that I have stressed in the texts to which you refer. How can one then attribute the *existence* of the hymen *properly* to woman? Not that it is any more the distinguishing feature of man or, for that matter, of the human creature. I would say the same for the term "invagination" which has, moreover, always been reinscribed in a chiasmus, one doubly folded, redoubled and inversed, etc.' (Derrida and McDonald, 1988: 181–2).

12 For a discussion of sonority compared with the reversibility of visibility see Wayne J. Froman (1990: 98–110).

13 Levinas does acknowledge a debt to Merleau-Ponty (Levinas, 1979: 205–6).

14 Dorothea E. Olkowski describes Merleau-Ponty's concept of existence as a concept which 'gives value to both body and consciousness and makes it possible for us to experience them together as an indistinguishable existential process operating in every human activity' (Olkowski, 1982–3).

15 For fuller discussions of this concept see Alphonso Lingis (1977; 1985: 58–73).

16 Elizabeth Grosz in turn comments on the sexual specificity of Lingis's description of the dissolution of the orgasmic body, which she argues is only the dissolution of the male body after the man's orgasm (Grosz, 1994: 110).

17 Elizabeth McMillan makes a similar criticism to Butler in her interpretation of Merleau-Ponty's discussion of sexuality, arguing that his discussion at first 'flirts with an interpretation of the sexed body which makes sexuality co-extensive with existence', but lapses into an objectivist perspective by describing himself as a painter-perceiver at the critical moment when he is trying to dissociate himself from such a position (McMillan, 1987). By way of contrast, Rosalyn Diprose suggests that Butler's conclusion that Merleau-Ponty's masculine subject is a disembodied voyeur is a little hasty when placed in the context of his broader discussion of Schneider. Diprose argues that Merleau-Ponty is concerned with the manner in which Schneider's general powers of objectification have been reduced

or altered rather than assuming that objectifying sexuality is the sole preserve of normal men (Diprose, forthcoming).

4 Vision in the flesh

1 For a discussion of the relationship between Merleau-Ponty's early attempts to grapple with the enigmas of perception and his later work on perception see Martin Jay (1993c: 143–85).

2 Merleau-Ponty discusses Cartesian optics in general in 'Eye and mind', in *The Primacy of Perception* (1964a: 169–78).

3 Dalia Judowitz demonstrates in detail how Descartes systematically undermines the role of vision and its perceptual domain in both his scientific and philosophical speculations (Judowitz, 1993: 63–86).

4 Jean-François Lyotard discusses Merleau-Ponty's application of this concept to Cézanne's painting. Lyotard is critical of Merleau-Ponty's analysis, observing that 'what is really at stake: to reveal what makes one see, and not what is visible . . . what was at stake for that painter was, in effect, to seize perception and render it at birth – perception "before" perception; the wonder of "it happening"' (Lyotard, 1984: 41).

5 The hyphenated spelling is Mark Taylor's (1987: 72).

6 See Michel Foucault, 'Man and His Doubles', in *The Order of Things* (1970: 303–43), and Gilles Deleuze, *Foucault* (1988: 58). For discussion of Foucault's criticism of, as well as influence by, Merleau-Ponty see Hubert L. Dreyfus and Paul Rabinow (1982); Martin Jay (1986: 184); and Richard A. Cohen (1984).

7 For an account of the correspondences between Foucault and Deleuze in their departure from representational approaches to the image see D. N. Rodowick (1990).

8 See Michel Foucault (1973a: 65–172).

9 I discuss this relationship to medical perceptions of the body more fully in 'The Mouth and the Clinical Gaze', in *Vital Signs* (forthcoming).

10 For discussion of the grotesque in relation to Bataille's pineal eye see Mark Taylor (1987: 115–48).

11 The blink is both a reflex action and an action which is to some extent within conscious control.

12 See 'The Child's Relations with Others', in *The Primacy of Perception and Other Essays* (Merleau-Ponty, 1964a: 96–155).

13 M. C. Dillon emphasizes Merleau-Ponty's theorizing of body-image in terms of a self-alienation which leads the infant out of a synchretic indeterminacy of self and other (Dillon, 1990: 14–26).

14 Merleau-Ponty and Lacan both posit the child's identification with the mirror image as the hinge which launches its entry into a world where it exists as an individual with others. Lacan posits the 'mirror stage' as a means of explaining the transition from auto-eroticism to object-love. In a reversal of Freud's conceptualization of an ego formation which makes narcissistic identification possible,

Lacan's 'mirror stage' posits the formation of an ideal ego which is itself the reflection of a narcissistic structure. The term *imago* is used to designate this reflected or imaginary double with which the infant identifies; internalizing as its own image the figure that it sees in the mirror. The *imago* is not the product of the infant's self-projection. It acts in a formative capacity, providing a *Gestalt* or form in which the infant integrates the multiple uncoordinated activities which animate it. Using this *imago*, the infant is able to represent its body to itself, thus establishing a locus for spatial orientation and mastery of the physical relationship between itself and other objects.

Lacan goes so far as to suggest that the *imago* is integrated at a neurological level in a mirror mapping process which occurs in the cerebral cortex. The mapping of an imaginary *Gestalt* rather than an anatomical one more adequately explains the symptoms of hysteria, phantom limb, and the exotic cleavages and reassemblages of body parts which are manifested in dreams. The imaginary *Gestalt* remains an entirely individual corporeal image which is resistant to symbolization, and pre-exists all social determination. It is the introjected personal phantasy on to which the child projects itself. However, it is an imaginary correspondence between an image and a real being, or the misrecognition and anticipation of a unity which cannot be actualized (Lacan, 1953; 1977: 1–7).

15 In his discussion of Merleau-Ponty's account of the specular body, John O'Neill suggests that the childhood game of 'peek-a-boo' is as much a game of mastery of presence and absence as Freud's 'Fort! Da!' (O'Neill, 1986: 211). However, I suggest that the 'peek-a-boo' game is a narcissistic play, while Freud's 'Fort! Da!' is a game of substitution, or means of representing presence and absence.

16 See Sigmund Freud, 'From the History of an Infantile Neurosis,' in *The Standard Edition of the Complete Psychological Works of Sigmund Freud*, Vol. 17 (1953: 1–122).

5 Touching flesh

1 Merleau-Ponty describes and extends Mauss's insights concerning the creation of social equivalences (Merleau-Ponty, 1974: 111–22).

2 'By the impossible, what ought one to have understood?

If we speak of it we will have to name something. Not to present the thing, here the impossible, but to try with its name, or with some name, to give an understanding of or to think this impossible thing, this impossible itself . . . it would not name what one thinks it names, to wit, the unity of a meaning that would be that of the gift' (Derrida, 1992: 169).

3 In Alphonso Lingis's translation of 'The Intertwining – The Chiasm' *lèvres* appears as 'laps'. In their translation of Irigaray's quotation from Merleau-Ponty's text Carolyn Burke and Gillian C. Gill correct this to 'lips', adding the comment that this typographical error 'seems to mime what Irigaray calls the invisibility of the feminine' (Irigaray, 1993a: 166). It is also possible that Lingis means 'lapses', which, while still justifying the translators' comment, would be a translation of Merleau-Ponty's expression that is closer to Irigaray's understanding of 'lips'.

4 See 'De Anima', *The Works of Aristotle*, Book II (2), 413b (1931).
5 Margaret Whitford gives an itemized explanation of the way in which Irigaray uses
the concept of the mucous repeatedly throughout her work (Whitford, 1991b:
102–3). The mucous is *interior*, always partly open, beyond control or closure. It
cannot be reduced to the *maternal-feminine* body and an attendant container-like
sexuality. The term indicates a body which is not easily incorporated into the male
imaginary, being neither exclusive to one sex nor a part-object separable from the
body. It is neither subject nor object, solid nor fluid. It expands and changes, but
not into a shape or readily visualized form. Irigaray defines the mucous as the
medium of the 'two lips', in which she articulates her controversial proposition of
female sexuality and women's speech.
6 For an outline of this history see Véronique Fóti (1990).
7 Jacques Derrida discusses the blink as an instant for reflection as 'the chance for
turning back on the very conditions of reflection, in all senses of that word, as if with
the help of a new optical device one could finally see sight' (Derrida, 1983: 19).
Derrida deconstructs this instant in 'Signs and the Blink of an Eye', in *Speech and
Phenomena and Other Essays on Husserl's Theory of Signs* (1973: 60–9). Derrida also
discusses the 'aperspective' of the retina in Merleau-Ponty's account of vision as an
analogical index of vision itself, that is: 'of that which, seeing itself see, is never-
theless not reflected, cannot be "thought" in the specular or speculative mode – and
thus is blinded because of this, blinded at this point of "narcissism", at that very
point where it sees itself looking' (1993: 53).
8 For a discussion of Derrida's argument that the structure of maternity disrupts
Reason's claim to self-sufficiency see Irene Harvey (1986: 209). For an interpretation of Derrida's account of maternal disruption of phallic law see Drucilla Cornell
(1991: 88–92).

6 Introduction to Levinas

1 As well as being considered in Derrida's essay 'Violence and Metaphysics: An Essay
on the Thought of Emmanuel Levinas', in *Writing and Difference* (1978: 79–153),
Levinas's associations with Husserl and Heidegger are discussed extensively by Edith
Wyschogrod (1974). Adriaan Peperzak has also undertaken such a task in his
introductory commentary (1993).
2 I have borrowed this mapping of the term for originary heteronomy from Edith
Wyschogrod (1980).
3 For an alignment of Irigaray's work with Levinas's see Elizabeth Grosz (1987; 1989:
140–83) and Tina Chanter (1995: 170–224).

7 Scintillating lighting

1 Edith Wyschogrod discusses Levinas's assessment of and break with Husserl's
ontology (1974: 27–50).
2 Martin Jay comments that Levinas conceives of the gaze as coming into being as a
pure avidity: 'Going beyond Debord's historical analysis of the society of the

spectacle, he insisted that vision itself was the root of the problem' (Jay, 1993a: 556). In my reading of Levinas vision is not a problem per se, but its avidity is the mark of its limited freedom.

3 See Georges Bataille, 'Rotten Sun', in *Visions of Excess* (1985: 57–8). Edith Wyschogrod discusses the difference between the two philosophers in relation to this sun (Wyschogrod, 1989: 194–5).

4 Alphonso Lingis uses the term 'sensitivity' to describe the exposure to alterity which paradoxically emerges within sensuous enjoyment (Lingis, 1986: 219–30).

5 See 'Phenomenon and Enigma', in *Collected Philosophical Papers* (Levinas, 1987a: 64).

6 Levinas defines and discusses *there is* as the phenomenon of impersonal being most succinctly in *Ethics and Infinity: Conversations with Philippe Nemo* (1985: 47–8).

7 See also Irene E. Harvey's discussion of Derrida's response to the Heideggerian principle of death (Harvey, 1986: 228–36).

8 Edith Wyschogrod discusses a range of misleading visual analogies which cling to Levinas's recruitment of the face as a visual equivalent for alterity, including some of those that have I referred to here (Wyschogrod, 1980: 179–203).

9 See Taylor (1987: 204–5) for a discussion of the trace in the work of a variety of post-Husserlian philosophers, and also a strict parallel between Levinas's and Kierkegaard's contrasting of singularity and individuality.

10 Levinas makes a distinction between strangeness and difference in response to a question about Derrida's interpretation of the face of the other as an alter ego which begins in the symmetry rather than dissymmetry of the ethical relation (Wright, Hughes and Ainsley 1988: 179).

11 See 'Meaning and Sense', in *Collected Philosophical Papers* (Levinas, 1987a: 102–7).

12 See Edith Wyschogrod (1980: 179–203).

13 As well as outlining the charge of phonocentrism directed at Levinas by both Derrida and Blanchot, Jill Robbins also discusses the necessity, in a philosophical tradition weighted towards the hermeneutical and the dialectical, to avoid the reduction of the face-to-face to the tranquil plenitude of a humanistic conversation (Robbins, 1991).

14 For a broader comparison see Susan Handelman (1991) and Peter Osborne (1995).

15 See Andrew Benjamin and Peter Osborne's introduction to *Walter Benjamin's Philosophy: Destruction and Experience* (1994: x–xiii).

16 Adriaan Peperzak emphasizes this theme in Levinas's work (Peperzak, 1993: 38–72).

17 See 'The Work of Art in the Age of Mechanical Reproduction', in *Illuminations* (Benjamin, 1968: 217–51).

18 Miriam Hansen comments: 'While Benjamin alludes to a phenomenological concept of the gaze, he above all invokes the romantic metaphor of nature opening its eyes . . . the notion . . . implies both a particular kind of attentiveness or receptivity (the human capability of responding to another's gaze, whether visual or intentional) and the actualization of this intersubjective experience in the relationship with non-human nature' (Hansen, 1987: 188).

19 See 'A Small History of Photography', in *One Way Street* (Benjamin, 1979: 240–57).

20 Benjamin develops the idea of an 'optical unconscious' from an essay by Siegfried Kracauer, 'Photography' (1927), reprinted, trans. Thomas Y. Levin (1993). I thank Jodi Brooks for directing me to this material.
21 Translation by Gyorgy Markus, in 'Excursion II: Walter Benjamin and the Commodity as Phantasmagoria', *Marxism & Theories of Culture* (Department of General Philosophy, University of Sydney), manuscript.

8 The lightness of touch

1 See translator's notes, *Anthropology from a Pragmatic Point of View* (Kant, 1974: 198–9).
2 As Lewis White Beck comments in the Preface to Kant's *Critique of Practical Reason*, touch is the paradigmatic sense of empiricism (Kant, 1956: 14).
3 By way of example of this phenomenon, a bumper sticker appeared in America in March 1993 which read 'The Most Dangerous Place in America to Live is in a Mother's Womb'. Isabelle Karpin discusses some legal implications of this construction of the maternal (Karpin, 1994).
4 This is a reference to Heidegger's account of authentic existence, which Levinas addresses in his analysis of the sensuousness of light (Levinas, 1987b: 70).
5 Levinas's most substantial exposition of the caress is in Section IV, B of *Totality and Infinity*, 'The Phenomenology of Eros' (1979: 256–66).
6 Edith Wyschogrod discusses the relationship between work and the groping hand in Levinas's work (Wyschogrod, 1989: 182–200). For a discussion of the hand's action of differentiation see also Jacques Derrida (1987: 161–96).
7 Tina Chanter maps the progressively more complex relationship between eroticism and ethical responsibility which develops chronologically in Levinas's work (Chanter, 1991: 130–46).

9 Illuminating passion

1 Gayatri Chakrvorty Spivak reads Irigaray's position on the radical undecidability of sexual difference as the daring of minimal alterity (Spivak, 1992: 76).
2 Emmanuel Levinas (1977), 'Et Dieu Créa la Femme', *Du sacré au saint*, Paris: Minuit, pp. 132–42, quoted by Derrida (1991b: 41).
3 *Ibid.*
4 Levinas does in fact speak of kissing, but as either an ambiguous grasping/being grasped (1981: 75) or as a simulation of devouring – more a love-bite (1978a: 43).
5 The mother–daughter relationship is the relationship, as Irigaray stresses, whose significance most eluded Freud, and the relationship whose non-signifiability most threatens women with psychosis (Whitford, 1986: 3–8).
6 In Lingis's translation of 'The Fecundity of the Caress', in *Face to Face with Levinas* (Cohen, 1986: 240), *enfantine* is rendered, with translator's licence, as 'infintile', suggesting a perverse infinite childhood.
7 For a detailed discussion of Irigaray's analysis of ontotheology see Penelope Deutscher (1994).

8 The remainder of sexual difference can be contrasted with a remainder that is the undifferentiable support of a single, masculine identity: 'If there is no more "earth" to press down/repress, to work, to represent, but also and always to desire (for one's own), no opaque matter which in theory does not know herself, then what pedestal remains for the ex-istence of the subject?' (Irigaray, 1985a: 133)

9 See 'Sorcerer Love: A Reading of Plato's *Symposium*, Diotima's Speech', in *An Ethics of Sexual Difference* (Irigaray, 1993a: 20–33). Irigaray discovers within the unfolding of Diotima's speech a form of love as a mediator of fecundity, which is excluded and passed over in the founding of an operative, teleological love of things and, ultimately, truth.

10 For a discussion of different phenomenological accounts of depth see Edward S. Casey (1991: 11). Irigaray explores the concept of elemental depth as a state of immersion in 'Speaking of Immemorial Waters', in *Marine Lover of Friedrich Nietzsche* (1991a: 1–73).

11 For an account that regards the two philosophers as being similar in this respect see Elizabeth Grosz (1987: 36–7).

12 The term 'sensitivity' as a form of sensibility is a nineteenth-century aesthetic term. Discussion of the political deployment of this humanist attribute is beyond the scope of my work here. However, for example, Sander Gilman describes the depiction of the sense of touch, conceptualized as the least discriminating of the senses, as the dominant sense of dark-skinned races and primitivism (1993: 198–224). The implication to be drawn from this assertion was that dark-skinned races had no aesthetic sensibility or refinement of taste. In using the term 'photosensitivity' I am emphasizing the extent to which Irigaray's conceptualization of touch might lend itself to a rereading of ideas of aesthetic sensibility.

13 The translators' note accompanying this section draws attention to Irigaray's emphasis on the root meaning of 'instance' as standing within the self, as opposed to 'ecstasy', which is a standing outside the self.

10 Conclusion

1 See 'The Pineal Eye' and 'The Solar Anus', in *Visions of Excess* (Bataille, 1985: 5–9 and 79–90).

2 For a discussion of the various strands of utopias dealt with in Irigaray's work see Margaret Whitford (1994). Moira Gatens questions the success with which Whitford argues against Irigaray's utopianism, claiming instead that Irigaray's deployment of a 'reality'/'imaginary' distinction sustains a contrast between an unsatisfactory present and idealized future (Gatens, 1996, p. ix). Jonathan Strauss describes Bataille's adaption of the plight of Icarus: 'Bataille stresses the indissociability of greatness and humiliation: as soon as the celestial overwhelms him, he becomes aware of his own abjection, and this single moment is described as a glorious self-perception. The moment of solar greatness is its opposite: the fall of Icarus, but an inverted fall of Icarus, who at his lowest moment – "the task I am pursuing" – is swept upwards in an act of self-immolation. Indeed, the fall of Icarus,

the futile expenditure of self in the raptures of freedom, which contrasts so fiercely with the science and self-preservation of his father, was already a sort of fall into the sun' (Strauss, 1990: 121).

3 Bataille makes this comment in relation to Bunuel's week-long sickness after filming the infamous eye-slitting scene in the surrealist film *Le Chien Andalou* (1928) (Bataille, 1985: 19n).

4 Gaston Bachelard analyses the ontological convertibility of radiation into matter and vice versa in contemporary physics. See 'Matter and Radiation', in *The New Scientific Spirit* (Bachelard, 1984: 61–84).

5 This difference is characterized by John Llewelyn as follows: 'whereas in Heidegger's analysis of *Dasein* the *sta* of the verb *stare* and *sistere* are prefixed by *ex-* or *ec-* to express the ways in which *Dasein* is ec-statically extended through time, in Levinas's analysis of subjectivity the *sta*, and so on, are prefixed by *in-*, as in instant' (Llewelyn, 1995: 26).

6 This comment is based on a longer discussion of some effects of digitization of the senses, including the fabrication of a sense of disembodiment in the virtual environment suit. See Vasseleu (1994).

7 See 'The Universal as Mediation', in *Sexes and Genealogies* (Irigaray, 1993b: 145).

Bibliography

Allen, Jeffner (1982–3) 'Through the Wild Region: An Essay in Phenomenological Feminism', *Review of Existential Psychology and Psychiatry* XVIII (1, 2 & 3): 241–59.

Aristotle (1931) 'De Anima', in W. D. Ross (ed.) *The Works of Aristotle*, Oxford: Clarendon Press.

Ashbaugh, Anne Freire (1978) 'The Philosophy of Flesh and the Flesh of Philosophy', *Research in Phenomenology* 8: 217–23.

Bachelard, Gaston (1984) *The New Scientific Spirit,* trans. Arthur Goldhammer, Boston: Beacon Press.

Bataille, Georges (1985) *Visions of Excess: Selected Writings, 1927–1939*, trans. Allan Stoekl, with Carl R. Lovitt and Donald Leslie, Jr, *Theory and History of Literature*, Vol. 14, Minneapolis: University of Minnesota Press.

Beauvoir, Simone de (1972) *The Second Sex*, trans. H. M. Parshley, Harmondsworth, Middlesex: Penguin.

Benjamin, Andrew and Osborne, Peter (eds) (1994) *Walter Benjamin's Philosophy: Destruction and Experience*, London and New York: Routledge.

Benjamin, Walter (1968) *Illuminations*, trans. Harry Zohn, New York: Schocken Books.

—— (1978) *Reflections*, trans. Edmund Jephcott, New York: Schocken Books.

—— (1979) *One Way Street*, trans. Edmund Jephcott and Kingsley Shorter, London: New Left Books.

—— (1982) *Das Passagen-Werk*, Vol. V (1), Frankfurt am Main: Suhrkamp Verlag.

Berry, Philippa (1994) 'The Burning Glass: Paradoxes of Feminist Revelation in *Speculum*', in Carolyn Burke, Naomi Schor and Margaret Whitford (eds) *Engaging with Irigaray: Feminist Philosophy and Modern European Thought*, New York: Columbia University Press.

Blanchot, Maurice (1981) *The Gaze of Orpheus and other literary essays*, trans. Lydia Davis, New York: Station Hill Press.

—— (1986) *The Writing of the Disaster*, trans. Ann Smock, Lincoln and London: University of Nebraska Press.

Blumenberg, Hans (1993) 'Light as a Metaphor for Truth: At the Preliminary Stage of

Philosophical Concept Formation', in David Michael Levin (ed.) *Modernity and the Hegemony of Vision*, Berkeley: University of California Press.

Butler, Judith (1989) 'Sexual Ideology and Phenomenological Description: A Feminist Critique of Merleau-Ponty's *Phenomenology of Perception*', in Jeffner Allen and Iris Marion Young (eds) *The Thinking Muse: Feminism and Modern French Philosophy*, Bloomington and Indianapolis: Indiana University Press.

—— (1990) *Gender Trouble: Feminism and the Subversion of Identity*, New York and London: Routledge.

—— (1993) *Bodies That Matter: On the Discursive Limits of 'Sex'*, New York and London: Routledge.

Caillois, Roger (1984) 'Mimicry and Legendary Psychasthenia', trans. John Shepley, *October* 31, Winter: 17–32.

Casey, Edward S. (1991) '"The Element of Voluminousness": Depth and Place Re-examined', in M. C. Dillon (ed.) *Merleau-Ponty Vivant*, Albany: State University of New York Press.

Chalier, Catherine (1991) 'Ethics and the Feminine', in Robert Bernasconi and Simon Critchley (eds) *Re-Reading Levinas*, Bloomington and Indianapolis: Indiana University Press.

Chanter, Tina (1991) 'Antigone's Dilemma', in Robert Bernasconi and Simon Critchley (eds) *Re-Reading Levinas*, Bloomington and Indianapolis: Indiana University Press.

—— (1995) *Ethics of Eros: Irigaray's Rewriting of the Philosophers*, New York and London: Routledge.

Cixous, Hélène (1980) 'Sorties', in Elaine Marks and Isabelle de Courtivron (eds) *New French Feminisms*, Brighton, Sussex: The Harvester Press.

Cohen, Richard A. (1984) 'Merleau-Ponty, the Flesh and Foucault', *Philosophy Today* 28, Winter: 329–38.

Cohen, Richard A. (ed.) (1986) *Face to Face with Levinas*, Albany: State University of New York Press.

Comay, Rebecca (1992) 'Framing Redemption: Aura, Origin, Technology in Benjamin and Heidegger', in Arleen B. Dallery and Charles. E. Scott (eds) *Ethics and Danger*, Albany: State University of New York Press.

Cornell, Drucilla (1991) *Beyond Accommodation: Ethical Feminism, Deconstruction and the Law*, New York and London: Routledge.

Crary, Jonathan (1990) *Techniques of the Observer: On Vision and Modernity in the Nineteenth Century*, Cambridge, Massachusetts and London, England: October Books, MIT Press.

Davies, Paul (1993) 'The Face and the Caress: Levinas's Ethical Alterations of Sensibility', in David Michael Levin (ed.) *Modernity and the Hegemony of Vision*, Berkeley: University of California Press.

Deleuze, Gilles (1988) *Foucault*, trans. Seàn Hand, Minneapolis: University of Minnesota Press.

Derrida, Jacques (1973) *Speech and Phenomena and Other Essays on Husserl's Theory of Signs*, trans. David B. Allison, Evanston: Northwestern University Press.

——— (1978) *Writing and Difference*, trans. Alan Bass, London and Henley: Routledge & Kegan Paul.

——— (1980) 'The Law of Genre,' *Glyph* 7: 202–32.

——— (1981a) *Dissemination*, trans. Barbara Johnson, Chicago: The University of Chicago Press.

——— (1981b) 'Economimesis', *Diacritics* 11, June: 3–25.

——— (1982) *Margins of Philosophy*, trans. Alan Bass, Brighton, Sussex: The Harvester Press.

——— (1983) 'The Principle of Reason: The University in the Eyes of Its Pupils', trans. Catherine Porter and Edward P. Morris, *Diacritics* 13(3) Fall: 3–20.

——— (1986) *Glas*, trans. John P. Leavey, Jr and Richard Rand, Lincoln and London: University of Nebraska Press.

——— (1987) '*Geschlecht* II: Heidegger's Hand', trans. John P. Leavey, Jr, in John Sallis (ed.) *Deconstruction and Philosophy: The Texts of Jacques Derrida*, Chicago and London: The University of Chicago Press.

——— (1991a) '"Eating Well", or the Calculation of the Subject: An Interview with Jacques Derrida', trans. Peter Connor and Avital Ronell, in Eduardo Cadava, Peter Connor, Jean-Luc Nancy (eds) *Who Comes after the Subject?*, New York and London: Routledge.

——— (1991b) 'At This Very Moment in This Work Here I Am', in Robert Bernasconi and Simon Critchley (eds) *Re-Reading Levinas*, Bloomington and Indianapolis: Indiana University Press.

——— (1992) 'Given Time: The Time of the King', trans. Peggy Kamuf, *Critical Inquiry* 18, Winter: 161–87.

——— (1993) *Memoirs of the Blind: The Self-Portrait and Other Ruins*, trans. Pascale-Anne Brault and Michael Naas, Chicago and London: The University of Chicago Press.

——— (1995) *On the Name*, trans. David Wood, John P. Leavey, Jr and Ian McLeod, Stanford: Stanford University Press.

Derrida, Jacques and McDonald, Christie (1988) 'Interview: Choreographies', *The Ear of the Other*, trans. Peggy Kamuf, Lincoln and London: University of Nebraska Press.

Descartes, René (1931) *The Philosophical Works of Descartes*, Vol. 1, trans. Elizabeth Haldane and G. R. T. Ross, Cambridge: Cambridge University Press.

Deutscher, Penelope (1994) 'Passing from the Man/God Schism to the Feminine-Divine (Irigaray on Divinity: From *Speculum* to *J'Aime à toi*)', *Hypatia* 9, 3, Fall: 88–111.

Dillon, M. C. (1988) *Merleau-Ponty's Ontology*, Bloomington and Indianapolis: Indiana University Press.

——— (1990) '*Ecart*: Reply to Lefort's "Flesh as Otherness"', in Galen A. Johnson and Michael B. Smith (eds) *Ontology and Alterity in Merleau-Ponty*, Evanston, Illinois: Northwestern University Press.

Dillon, M. C. (ed.) (1990) *Merleau-Ponty Vivant*, Albany: State University of New York Press.

Diprose, Rosalyn (1994) *The Bodies of Women: Ethics, Embodiment and Sexual Difference*, London and New York: Routledge.

—— (forthcoming) 'Generosity: Between Love and Desire', *Hypatia*.

Dreyfus, Hubert L. and Rabinow, Paul (1982) *Michel Foucault: Beyond Structuralism and Hermeneutics,* Brighton, Sussex: The Harvester Press.

Flynn, Bernard Charles (1984) 'Textuality and the Flesh: Derrida and Merleau-Ponty', *Journal of the British Society for Phenomenology* 15(2) May: 164–79.

Fóti, Véronique M. (1990) 'The Dimension of Color', *International Studies in Philosophy* 22(3): 13–28.

Foucault, Michel (1970) *The Order of Things: An Archaeology of the Human Sciences,* New York: Vintage Books.

—— (1973a) *The Birth of the Clinic: An Archaeology of Medical Perception,* trans. A. M. Sheridan Smith, New York: Pantheon Books.

—— (1973b) *Madness and Civilization: A History of Insanity in the Age of Reason,* trans. Richard Howard, New York: Vintage Books.

—— (1977) 'Nietzsche, Genealogy, History', in Donald F. Bouchard (ed.) *Language, Counter-Memory, Practice,* Ithaca, New York: Cornell University Press.

Frankel, Eugene (1976) 'Corpuscular Optics and the Wave Theory of Light: The Science and Politics of a Revolution in Physics', *Social Studies of Science* 6: 141–84.

Freud, Sigmund (1953) 'From the History of an Infantile Neurosis', *The Standard Edition of the Complete Psychological Works of Sigmund Freud,* Vol. 17, trans. J. Strachey, London: The Hogarth Press.

Froman, Wayne J. (1990) 'Alterity and the Paradox of Being', in Galen A. Johnson and Michael B. Smith (eds) *Ontology and Alterity in Merleau-Ponty,* Evanston, Illinois: Northwestern University Press.

Fuss, Diana J. (1989) 'Essentially Speaking: Luce Irigaray's Language of Essence', *Hypatia* 3(3), Winter: 62–80.

Gashé, Rodolphe (1986) *The Tain of the Mirror: Derrida and the Philosophy of Reflection,* Cambridge, Massachusetts and London: Harvard University Press.

Gatens, Moira (1991) *Feminism and Philosophy: Perspectives on Difference and Equality,* Cambridge: Polity Press.

—— (1996) *Imaginary Bodies: Ethics, Power and Corporeality,* London and New York: Routledge.

Gilman, Sander (1993) 'Touch, Sexuality and Disease', in W. F. Bynum and Roy Porter (eds) *Medicine and the Five Senses,* Cambridge: Cambridge University Press.

Grosz, Elizabeth (1987) 'The "People of the Book": Representation and Alterity in Emmanuel Levinas', *Art & Text* 26, September–November: 32–40.

—— (1989) *Sexual Subversions: Three French Feminists,* Sydney: Allen & Unwin.

—— (1993) 'Merleau-Ponty and Irigaray in the Flesh', *Thesis Eleven* 36: 37–59.

—— (1994) *Volatile Bodies: Toward a Corporeal Feminism,* Bloomington and Indianapolis: Indiana University Press, and Sydney: Allen & Unwin.

Handelman, Susan (1982) *The Slayers of Moses: The Emergence of Rabbinic Interpretation in Modern Literary Theory,* Albany: State University of New York Press.

—— (1991) *Fragments of Redemption: Jewish Thought and Literary Theory in Benjamin, Sholem, and Levinas,* Bloomington and Indianapolis: Indiana University Press.

Hansen, Miriam (1987) 'Benjamin, Cinema and Experience: "The Blue Flower in the Land of Technology"', *New German Critique* 40, Winter: 179–224.

Harvey, Irene (1986) *Derrida and the Economy of Différance*, Bloomington: Indiana University Press.

Heidegger, Martin (1961) *An Introduction to Metaphysics*, trans. Ralph Manheim, Garden City, NY: Doubleday.

—— (1977a) *Basic Writings*, ed. David Farrell Krell, San Francisco: Harper & Row.

—— (1977b) 'The Question Concerning Technology', *The Question Concerning Technology and Other Essays*, trans. William Lovitt, New York: Harper & Row.

Holland, Nancy J. (1986) 'Merleau-Ponty on Presence: A Derridean Reading', *Research in Phenomenology* 16: 111–20.

Irigaray, Luce (1985a) *Speculum of the Other Woman*, trans. Gillian C. Gill, Ithaca, New York: Cornell University Press.

—— (1985b) *This Sex Which Is Not One*, trans. Catherine Porter, Ithaca, New York: Cornell University Press.

—— (1991a) *Marine Lover of Friedrich Nietzsche*, trans. Gillian C. Gill, New York: Columbia University Press.

—— (1991b) 'Questions to Emmanuel Levinas: On the Divinity of Love', trans. in Robert Bernasconi and Simon Critchley (eds) *Re-Reading Levinas*, Bloomington and Indianapolis: Indiana University Press.

—— (1992) *Elemental Passions*, trans. Joanne Collie and Judith Still, London: The Athlone Press.

—— (1993a) *An Ethics of Sexual Difference*, trans. Carolyn Burke and Gillian C. Gill, Ithaca, New York: Cornell University Press.

—— (1993b) *Sexes and Genealogies*, trans. Gillian C. Gill, New York: Columbia University Press.

—— (1993c) *je, tu, nous: Towards a Culture of Difference*, trans. Alison Martin, New York and London: Routledge.

Jardine, Alice A. (1985) *Gynesis: Configurations of Woman and Modernity*, Ithaca, New York: Cornell University Press.

Jay, Martin (1986) 'In the Empire of the Gaze: Foucault and the Denigration of Vision in Twentieth-century French Thought', in David Couzens Hoy (ed.) *Foucault: A Critical Reader*, Oxford: Basil Blackwell.

—— (1993a) *Downcast Eyes: The Denigration of Vision in Twentieth-Century French Thought*, Berkeley: University of California Press.

—— (1993b) *Force Fields: Between Intellectual History and Cultural Critique*, New York and London: Routledge.

—— (1993c) 'Sartre, Merleau-Ponty and the Search for a New Ontology of Sight', in David Michael Levin (ed.) *Modernity and the Hegemony of Vision*, Berkeley: University of California Press.

Jonas, Hans (1954) 'The Nobility of Sight', *Philosophy and Phenomenological Research* 14(4). Reprinted in Stuart Spicker (ed.) *The Philosophy of the Body: Rejections of Cartesian Dualism*, New York: Quadrangle/New York Times, 1970.

Judowitz, Dalia (1993) 'Vision, Representation and Technology', in David Michael

Levin (ed.) *Modernity and the Hegemony of Vision*, Berkeley: University of California Press.

Kant, Immanuel (1956) *Critique of Practical Reason*, trans. Lewis White Beck, New York: Macmillan Publishing Company.

—— (1974) *Anthropology from a Pragmatic Point of View*, trans. Mary J. Gregor, The Hague: Martinus Nijhoff.

Karpin, Isabelle (1994) 'Reimagining Maternal Selfhood: Transgressing the Body Boundaries and the Law', *Australian Feminist Law Journal* 2, March: 36–62.

Keenan, Thomas (1993) 'Windows: Of Vulnerability', in Bruce Robbins (ed.) *The Phantom Public Sphere*, Minneapolis and London: University of Minnesota Press.

Keller, Evelyn Fox and Grontkowski, Christine R. (1983) 'The Mind's Eye', in Sandra Harding and Merrill B. Hintikka (eds) *Discovering Reality*, Dordrecht: D. Reidel Publishing Company.

Kracauer, Siegfried (1993) 'Photography' (1927), trans. Thomas Y. Levin, *Critical Inquiry*, 19(3): 421–36.

Krauss, Rosalind E. (1993) *The Optical Unconscious*, Cambridge, Massachusetts and London: October Books, MIT Press.

Lacan, Jacques (1953) 'Some Reflections on the Ego', *International Journal of Psycho-analysis* 34: 11–17.

—— (1977) *Écrits: A Selection*, trans. A. Sheridan, London: Tavistock Publications.

—— (1979) *The Four Fundamental Concepts of Psychoanalysis*, trans. Alan Sheridan, Harmondsworth, Middlesex: Penguin Books.

Lefort, Claude (1990) 'Flesh and Otherness', in Galen A. Johnson and Michael B. Smith (eds) *Ontology and Alterity in Merleau-Ponty*, Evanston, Illinois: Northwestern University Press.

Levinas, Emmanuel (1969) 'Judaism and the Feminine Element', trans. Edith Wyschogrod, *Judaism* 18, 1: 30–8.

—— (1978a) *Existence and Existents*, trans. Alphonso Lingis, Dordrecht, Boston, London: Kluwer Academic Publishers.

—— (1978b) 'Signature', trans. Mary Ellen Petrisko, in Adrian Peperzak (ed.) *Research in Phenomenology* 8: 175–89.

—— (1979) *Totality and Infinity: An Essay on Exteriority*, trans. Alphonso Lingis, Pittsburgh: Duquesne University Press.

—— (1981) *Otherwise Than Being or Beyond Essence*, trans. Alphonso Lingis, The Hague: Martinus Nijhoff.

—— (1985) *Ethics and Infinity: Conversations with Philippe Nemo*, trans. Richard A. Cohen, Pittsburgh: Duquesne University Press.

—— (1986a) 'The Trace of the Other', trans. Alphonso Lingis, in M. Taylor (ed.) *Deconstruction in Context*, Chicago: University of Chicago Press.

—— (1986b) 'Dialogue with Emmanuel Levinas', in Richard A. Cohen (ed.) *Face to Face with Levinas*, Albany: State University of New York Press.

—— (1987a) *Collected Philosophical Papers*, trans. Alphonso Lingis, Dordrecht, Boston and Lancaster: Martinus Nijhoff.

—— (1987b) *Time and the Other*, trans. Richard A. Cohen, Pittsburgh, Pennsylvania: Duquesne University Press.

—— (1988) 'Useless Suffering', in Robert Bernasconi and David Wood (eds) *The Provocation of Levinas*, London and New York: Routledge.

—— (1990a) 'Sensibility', trans. Michael B. Smith, in Galen A. Johnson and Michael B. Smith (eds) *Ontology and Alterity in Merleau-Ponty*, Evanston, Illinois: Northwestern University Press.

—— (1990b) 'Intersubjectivity: Notes on Merleau-Ponty', trans. Michael B. Smith, in Galen A. Johnson and Michael B. Smith (eds) *Ontology and Alterity in Merleau-Ponty*, Evanston, Illinois: Northwestern University Press.

—— (1991) 'Wholly Otherwise', in Robert Bernasconi and Simon Critchley (eds) *Re-Reading Levinas*, Bloomington and Indianapolis: Indiana University Press.

Libertson, Joseph (1982) *Proximity: Levinas, Blanchot, Bataille and Communication*, The Hague, Boston and London: Martinus Nijhoff.

Lindberg, David C. (1976) *Theories of Vision from Al-Kindi to Kepler*, Chicago and London: Chicago University Press.

Lingis, Alphonso (1977) 'Sense and Non-Sense in the Sexed Body', *Cultural Hermeneutics* 4: 344–65.

—— (1985) *Libido: The French Existential Theories*, Bloomington: Indiana University Press.

—— (1986) 'The Sensuality and the Sensitivity', in Richard A. Cohen (ed.) *Face to Face with Levinas*, Albany: State University of New York Press.

—— (1991) 'Imperatives', in M. C. Dillon (ed.) *Merleau-Ponty Vivant*, Albany: State University of New York Press.

—— (1994) *Foreign Bodies*, New York and London: Routledge.

Llewelyn, John (1995) *Emmanuel Levinas: The Genealogy of Ethics*, London and New York: Routledge.

Lyotard, Jean-François (1978) 'One of the Things at Stake in Women's Struggles', trans. D. J. Clark, W. Woodhill and J. Mowitt, *Sub-Stance* 20: 9–17.

—— (1984) 'The Sublime and the Avant-Garde', *Artforum* 22(8), April: 36–43.

—— (1991) *Phenomenology*, trans. Brian Beakley, Albany: State University of New York Press.

McMillan, Elizabeth (1987) 'Female Difference in the Texts of Merleau-Ponty', *Philosophy Today* 31(4), Winter: 359–66.

Madison, Gary Brent (1990) 'Flesh as Otherness', in Galen A. Johnson and Michael B. Smith (eds), *Ontology and Alterity in Merleau-Ponty*, Evanston, Illinois: Northwestern University Press.

Markus, Gyorgy (forthcoming) *Marxism and Theories of Culture*, manuscript, Department of General Philosophy, University of Sydney.

Mauss, Marcel (1969) *The Gift: Forms and Functions of Exchange in Archaic Societies*, trans. Ian Cunnison, London: Cohen & West Ltd.

Merleau-Ponty, Maurice (1960) *Signes*, Paris: Gallimard.

—— (1962) *The Phenomenology of Perception*, trans. Colin Smith, London and Henley: Routledge & Kegan Paul.

—— (1963) *The Structure of Behaviour*, trans. Alden L. Fisher, Boston: Beacon Press.

—— (1964a) James M. Edie (ed.) *The Primacy of Perception and Other Essays*, Evanston, Illinois: Northwestern University Press.

—— (1964b) *Sense and Non-Sense*, trans. Hubert L. Dreyfus and Patricia Allen Dreyfus, Evanston, Illinois: Northwestern University Press.

—— (1964c) *Signs*, trans. Richard C. McCleary, Evanston, Illinois: Northwestern University Press.

—— (1968) *The Visible and the Invisible*, trans. Alphonso Lingis, Evanston, Illinois: Northwestern University Press.

—— (1974) 'From Mauss to Claude Lévi-Strauss', in John O'Neill (ed.) *Phenomenology, Language and Sociology: Selected Essays of Maurice Merleau-Ponty*, London: Heinemann.

Nietzsche, Friedrich (1969) *On the Genealogy of Morals*, trans. Walter Kaufmann and R. J. Hollingdale, New York: Vintage Books.

—— (1973) *Beyond Good and Evil*, trans. R. J. Hollingdale, Harmondsworth, Middlesex: Penguin.

Nye, Andrea (1993) 'Assisting at the Birth and Death of Philosophic Vision', in David Michael Levin (ed.) *Modernity and the Hegemony of Vision*, Berkeley: University of California Press.

O'Neill, John (1986) 'The Specular Body: Merleau-Ponty and Lacan on Infant Self and Other', *Synthese* 66: 201–17.

Olkowski, Dorothea E. (1982–3) 'Merleau-Ponty's Freudianism: From the Body of Consciousness to the Body of Flesh', *Review of Existential Psychology and Psychiatry* XVIII (1, 2 & 3): 97–116.

Osborne, Peter (1995) *The Politics of Time: Modernity and Avant-Garde,* London and New York: Verso.

Paulson, William R. (1987) *Enlightenment, Romanticism, and the Blind in France*, Princeton, New Jersey: Princeton University Press.

Peperzak, Adriaan (1993) *To the Other — An Introduction to the Philosophy of Emmanuel Levinas*, West Lafayette, Indiana: Purdue University Press.

Place, James Gordon (1976) 'The Painting and the Natural Thing in the Philosophy of Merleau-Ponty', *Cultural Hermeneutics* 4: 75–91.

Plato (1955) *The Republic*, trans. Desmond Lee, Harmondsworth, Middlesex: Penguin Books.

Polan, Dana (1988) 'Powers of Vision, Visions of Power', *camera obscura* 18, September: 106–19.

Robbins, Jill (1991) '*Visage, Figure*: Reading Levinas's *Totality and Infinity*', *Yale French Studies* 79: 135–49.

Rodowick, D. N. (1990) 'Reading the Figural', *camera obscura* 24, September: 11–44.

Ronchi, Vasco (1957) *Optics: The Science of Vision*, trans. Edward Rosen, New York: New York University Press.

—— (1970) *The Nature of Light: An Historical Survey*, trans. V. Barocas, London: Heinemann.

Sartre, Jean-Paul (1958) *Being and Nothingness*, trans. Hazel E. Barnes, London: Methuen & Co Ltd.

Sobchack, Vivian (1992) *The Address of the Eye: A Phenomenology of Film Experience*, Princeton, New Jersey: Princeton University Press.

Sofoulis, Zoe (1988) *Through the Lumen: Frankenstein and the Optics of Re-origination*, PhD dissertation, University of California at Santa Cruz.

Spivak, Gayatri Chakravorty (1983) 'Displacement and the Discourse of Woman', in Mark Krupnick (ed.) *Displacement: Derrida and After*, Bloomington: Indiana University Press.

—— (1987) *In Other Worlds: Essays in Cultural Politics*, New York and London: Methuen.

—— (1989) 'Feminism and Deconstruction, Again: Negotiating with Unacknowledged Masculinism', in Teresa Brennan (ed.) *Between Feminism and Psychoanalysis*, London and New York: Routledge.

—— (1992) 'French Feminism Revisited: Ethics and Politics', in Judith Butler and Joan W. Scott (eds) *Feminists Theorize the Political*, New York and London: Routledge.

Strauss, Jonathan (1990) 'The Inverted Icarus', *Yale French Studies* 78: 106–23.

Stenstad, Gail (1993) 'Merleau-Ponty's Logos: The Sensing of Flesh', *Philosophy Today* 37(1), Spring: 52–61.

Stewart, Susan (1993) *On Longing: Narratives of the Miniature, the Gigantic, the Souvenir, the Collection*, Durham and London: Duke University Press.

Taylor, Mark (1987) *Altarity*, Chicago and London: The University of Chicago Press.

Vasseleu, Cathryn (1991) 'The face before the mirror stage', *Hypatia* 6(3) Fall: 140–55.

—— (1994) 'Virtual Bodies/Virtual Worlds', *Australian Feminist Studies* 19, May: 155–69.

—— (1996) 'Patent Pending: Laws of Invention, Animal Life-forms, and Bodies as Ideas', in Pheng Cheah, David Frazer and Judith Grbish (eds) *Thinking Through the Body of the Law*, Sydney: Allen & Unwin.

—— (forthcoming) 'The Mouth and the Clinical Gaze', in Janet Price and Margrit Shildrick (eds) *Vital Signs: Feminist Reconfigurations of the Bio/Logical Body*, Edinburgh: Edinburgh University Press.

Virilio, Paul (1993) 'The Third Interval: A Critical Transition', in Verena Andermatt Conley (ed.) on behalf of the Miami Theory Collective *Rethinking Technologies*, Minneapolis and London: University of Minnesota Press.

Whitford, Margaret (1986) 'Luce Irigaray and the Female Imaginary: Speaking as a Woman', *Radical Philosophy*, Summer: 3–8.

—— (1991a) *Philosophy in the Feminine*, London and New York: Routledge.

—— (1991b) 'Irigaray's Body Symbolic', *Hypatia* 6(3), Fall: 192–203.

—— (1994) 'Irigaray, Utopia and the Death Drive', in Carolyn Burke, Naomi Schor and Margaret Whitford (eds) *Engaging with Irigaray: Feminist Philosophy and Modern European Thought*, New York: Columbia University Press.

Wright, Tamra, Hughes, Peter, Ainsley, Alison (1988) 'The Paradox of Morality: An Interview with Emmanuel Levinas', in Robert Bernasconi and David Wood (eds) *The Provocation of Levinas*, London and New York: Routledge.

Wyschogrod, Edith (1974) *Emmanuel Levinas: The Problem of Ethical Metaphysics*, The Hague: Martinus Nijhoff.

—— (1980) 'Doing before Hearing', in François Laruelle (ed.) *Textes pour Emmanuel Lévinas*, Paris: Jean-Michel Place.

—— (1989) 'Derrida, Levinas, and Violence', in Hugh J. Silverman (ed.) *Derrida and Deconstruction, Continental Philosophy II*, New York and London: Routledge.

—— (1992) 'Does Continental Ethics Have a Future?', in Arleen B. Dallery and Charles E. Scott with P. Holley Roberts (eds) *Ethics and Danger: Essays on Heidegger and Continental Thought*, Albany: State University of New York Press.

Young, Iris Marion (1985) 'Pregnant Subjectivity and the Limits of Existential Phenomenology', in D. Idhe and D. H. Silverman (eds) *Descriptions*, Albany: State University of New York Press.

—— (1990) *Throwing like a Girl and Other Essays in Feminist Philosophy and Social Theory*, Bloomington and Indianapolis: Indiana University Press.

Yount, Mark (1990) 'Two Reversibilities: Merleau-Ponty and Derrida', *Philosophy Today* 34, Summer: 129–40.

Index